THE OTHER SIDE OF THE COUNTER

Seven Years Running a Village Shop in Somerset

This account is based on the memories of Sue and Keith Gudgeon, the owners of The Village Shop, Charlton Horethorne, from 1996 to 2003.

Our memories are not infallible so we apologise to the residents of Charlton Horethorne for any inaccuracies they may spot, they are not intentional !!

In the unlikely event that any profits are made from the sale of this book, they will be given to charity !

DORSET COUNTY LIBRARY, HQ

2 2 NOV 2008

First published in 2008 by Sue Gudgeon

All rights reserved. No part of this book maybe reproduced in any form or by any means without permission in writing from the publisher.

Copyright © 2008 *Sue Gudgeon*

ISBN 978-0-9559377-0-5

Printed by Remous Limited, Milborne Port, Dorset DT9 5EP
www.remous.com

Front cover photo:
The Village Shop post-refurbishment in the late 1990's

Back cover photo:
One of the earliest photographs of the Village Shop in Charlton Horethorne – known to be prior to 1905 as there is no telegraph pole outside the shop!

This book is dedicated to my partner, in every sense of the word, Keith, without whom this whole adventure would not have been possible, to our families who, at times, thought we had gone completely mad and to the people of Charlton Horethorne who have so enriched our lives since we arrived in this beautiful part of the world.

CONTENTS

In the Beginning	9
We Take the Plunge	13
January 1996	15
February 1996	18
March 1996	20
April 1996	23
May 1996	30
June 1996	37
Prior to opening	42
The Opening	49
Village Involvement – Or How We Never Said No!	57
Help is at Hand	63
New and Changing Suppliers	68
Arts and Crafts	73
Fun with the Customers	79
Local Suppliers	87
Home Life	90
Christmas	95
Some of the Boring Bits!	98
New Services	105
The Good, the Bad and the Sad	108
Post Office	113
Clouds in the Sky	119
New Suppliers and the Challenge of Being a Newsagent	129
Innovations and Replacements	134
Village Events	136
Outstanding Occasions – of One Sort and Another	140
Hitting the Headlines	148
Selling Up and Moving On	150
Postscript	155
The Known History of Charlton Horethorne Village Shop and Post Office	156

In the Beginning

We had talked about running our own business. Keith was due to take early retirement as the General Manager of an insurance company and my contract as a Human Resources Consultant was coming to an end. We had done the life of commuting on trains, writing interminable papers and Board reports and attending increasingly tedious and repetitive meetings. We were well paid but it never seemed that our efforts bore any relationship to the pay we, or others, received and we were constantly at the beck and call of people for whom we had diminishing respect.

But what to do? Whatever we talked about seemed to have as many pitfalls as attractions and sometimes it seemed easier to fall back on our existing professions. More comfortable, less risky – but would we regret it?

Then I saw it. The road from London to the West Country, after you turn off the M3, is a series of dashing dual carriageways interspersed with frustrating, if scenic, stretches of single carriageway. Somehow designed to keep you in your place. A reasonable run of dual carriageway by-passes the Somerset town of Wincanton and off this section is a turning to the historic market town of Sherborne, some 7 miles further south. I could do this road in my sleep as my parents lived in Sherborne and my son was at school in Taunton, so it was very familiar territory.

The road to Sherborne passes through the village of Charlton Horethorne, nestling under Charn Hill, with views across the Blackmore Vale. In its centre, the road skirts the village green, the other side of which stands the Kings Arms pub and the village shop. Or at least, on that day when I spotted it, the Cinderella of village shops with an equally sad looking cottage next door and a very large 'For Sale' notice. An idea began to form in my mind.

Unbeknown to anyone, I contacted the agent and made arrangements to look around on my way back to London on the Monday morning. The young lady who met me at the property viewed me with an air of sympathy and incredulity as she took me firstly into the shop. The owner of the property was elderly and lived a few miles away and she had put it on the market after the last of a succession of tenants had failed to make the business pay. In order not to lose what little was left of the service provided by the shop, a committee was formed and a team of volunteers from the village had kept it going whilst it was for sale, with the help of a local postmistress who came twice a week to provide Post Office facilities.

It is difficult to describe how bad things were in the shop or convey the stalwart nature of the volunteers who were coping with it. The shop gave the impression of a poorly maintained village hall with a variety of shop fittings suitable for a 1950's auction room and a stock of minimal proportions. There was a huge atrium-style sky-light in the centre of the ceiling which, on wet days, leaked copiously into anything up to nine buckets strategically placed around the floor. The glass in one of the main shop windows was cracked and a net curtain of dubious age had been placed over it. The Post Office at the back had been broken into in the recent past and was therefore not usable. The back storeroom had Acro props holding up the roof and one ventured in at one's peril. The lighting was very poor and there was no heating – the volunteers huddled around gas heaters, which gave off heat to about a two foot radius and made the shop smell like a mobile camp kitchen. And in the middle of all this the volunteers maintained a skeleton (almost literally) service with a humour reminiscent of the dark days of the War.

But it was there. The potential. The shop was large, it was on a busy through road and the village had proved it wanted a shop. I was hooked. I was not really listening to what the girl from the estate agent was saying, plans were already beginning to form in my mind. Then we moved into the cottage.

This could be accessed via a door in the shop and we entered a corridor housing cardboard boxes, brooms and buckets and the cold and the damp hit us. To my left were two windows looking out onto the garden – or they would have been if I could have seen through the condensation running down them – and to my right was a double doorway into the lounge. Straight ahead was a full-frontal view of the downstairs toilet – tinned-salmon pink with art-deco type fittings. The lounge was quite a plain room with a thirty year old, dusky blue, tiled fireplace, two alcove cupboards, one with the door hanging off, a beam encased in black-painted plywood and another dripping window looking out to the small front garden. This was primarily paved, with an ivy-clad wall and, most curiously, an ancient hip-bath on four feet, full of dead geraniums.

Out into the entrance hall and the jewel in the crown faced me. The most beautifully carved walnut banister swirled upwards with the curving staircase. How could something of such beauty survive in this decaying desolation? The dining room was similar to the lounge but it benefited from an attractive, although dirty, Minster fireplace. However, the addition of a hanging rail in the recess to the right of the fireplace, when the room had been used as a downstairs bedroom, did nothing to accentuate the room's potential.

The downstairs bathroom, in the same tinned salmon pink as the loo, had similar art-deco type fittings and, if you like that sort of thing, was well appointed when compared with the rest of the cottage. Particularly, the kitchen. The kitchen! It was almost indescribable. In one corner there was the hot water tank with all the lagging lying in pieces around it like a fall of autumn leaves. Some of the ceiling had come down over the sink whilst other pieces hung like a menacing potential avalanche. And there, in the middle of the floor, was the safe from the shop! The side had been cut into, sardine-tin fashion, and the contents removed leaving a vicious metallic wound.

"And this would be the utility room", the agent bravely continued as we stepped up into a lean-to stone outhouse suitable for a nativity scene.

Looking up, I saw the rafters, tiles and glimpses of sky whilst on the walls were a cold tap and an electric light switch saying 'Dangerous, do not touch!'

Nothing daunted we went upstairs, the silky smooth walnut of the banister restoring my slightly challenged enthusiasm. Into the main bedroom, which yielded the surprise of an immaculate polished wood floor – an oasis of sophistication in a sea of decrepitude. The two, damp, French windows opened onto a balcony which looked west over the tundra otherwise known as the garden but again hope sprung eternal as I glimpsed what looked like a glorious view down a hidden, winding valley beyond the wall at the bottom of the jungle. The bedroom spanned the depth of the house and opposite the French windows was a small, original cottage window, barely six inches off the floor but set in a wonderful, thick, comforting wall about fifteen inches deep and with a view through the old wobbly glass over the village green.

"This could be converted into an en-suite shower room", my tremulous guide suggested as we looked into a reasonably sized loo of very strange décor.

Apart from the fact that this room could be accessed from the landing as well as the bedroom, giving certain privacy problems, the most startling thing about it was the extraordinary combination of colours. Not only was the toilet pan a different colour from the seat and the seat a different colour from the cistern – an unusual combination of turquoise, aubergine and green – but the whole ensemble had been brought together with wallpaper combining these colours in a series of Olympic rings. To compound the unusual appearance of the room, the loo itself had been built up on wooden blocks about three inches high. This was something to do with improving the drop in the drainage, I was informed, and I decided I did not want to enquire any more deeply into these technicalities.

On then to the second bedroom which was as large as the first but in nothing like such good condition as its predecessor – an enormous patch of damp in the corner by the door had resulted in part of the ceiling coming down to reveal the ceiling laths. There was also a fireplace in the far wall, which looked as though it had had a succession of nesting birds depositing their spare housing materials – and droppings for that matter – down it. Still, it was a large room with potential. That word again.

Lastly we wound our way around the corridor to the third bedroom and, in the course of this manoeuvre, I found the first real stumbling block. Keith is six foot five inches tall and to get to the third bedroom required me to almost duck to get under the lintel, which formed the original outer wall of the cottage. Still, I rationalised, he would not have to come around here very much, particularly if this was a spare bedroom. Spare bedroom was a grandiose title for what met me around the corner. On the floor was a rolled up, damp and rather unpleasant looking carpet. Again all the wallpaper was hanging off the walls because of dampness but the most curious item in the room was the window. This was a metal framed, double window but one opening hinged outwards from the room and one hinged inwards. The reason for this became clear when I rubbed a viewing hole in the condensation. Beyond the window which opened inwards was a drain-pipe taking water off the roof but rather than going straight downwards to a drain, it ran down in front of the window and then disappeared through the house at downstairs ceiling level. Very curious.

"Would you like to look outside?", my agent asked timidly.

"Oh, yes please," I replied and she looked slightly startled.

Out through the kitchen door and we were in a paved courtyard – a real suntrap on a nice day – off which led some steps up to the garden. It is very difficult to describe how awful this was. The terracing between the patio and the rest of the garden was a combination of stone and red brick and was completely overgrown. The steps up to the garden were quite extraordinary, home-made, concrete steps, curved at the front, of varying pitches and depths and, quite dangerously, in wet weather, constructed so that the treads had smooth, curving fronts to them. It was rather like trying to walk up and down one of those stepped water slides you find at adventure parks.

Beyond the steps was a jungle. There appeared to be several large and quite elderly fruit trees around the perimeter, a number of self-seeded elder trees, a large and dominating eucalyptus and endless ivy, nettles and couch grass. The garden was obviously longer than it was wide but it was impossible to totally gauge its boundaries or to get a better idea of the view I had glimpsed from the bedroom. On the northern side of the garden was a building running two thirds of its length, which was accessible by a side door. This was the garage.

Double length, rather than double width, garages are not the most convenient but it still would provide room for the car and excellent storage space. At least it would be excellent when the roof, which was leaking and beginning to subside, was repaired and it had a main door. This would ensure that whatever wildlife was currently using the garage as a toilet made other arrangements. The reason there was no door was that there was one further down the drive. Drive is a rather grandiose term for the concreted access from the road which ran up the side of the cottage, adjacent to the next door farmyard, to the garage. At the road end of this accessway, a carport had been formed by roofing the drive over for a stretch of about twenty feet with corrugated iron and putting an up-and-over door on the front. This whole area, which had the side of the cottage on one side and a one and a half metre high breeze block wall on the other, got virtually no sun and was damp, green with algae and altogether rather unpleasant. But it had potential.

"Thank you. That was very interesting," I said. "I would like to think about it and discuss it with my partner."

"Fine," said my agent. "We look forward to hearing from you."

She sounded as convincing as someone who says they do not mind going to the dentist! But little did she know, I was hooked. I rang Keith and told him what I had done and he patiently indulged me by saying he would come and have a look. We wanted a challenge to face together but I had a feeling that he thought that this was a shade too challenging. Anyway, I made us another appointment to view and, in the meantime, my mind was a frenzy of ideas – walls to move, décor to plan, lifestyle to look forward to. And not least of all, how we would run a shop. Yes, how do you run a shop?! Lots of people did it so it couldn't be that difficult –but how did you do it? What did you stock, where did you get it from, how did you price it etc. etc. etc. But these were mere details in an exciting project and I could not get further than the excitement!

We Take the Plunge

Luckily it was a fine sunny day when I met Keith off the train from London and drove him to Charlton Horethorne. Looking back on it I think I probably wittered on endlessly trying to balance all the possibilities of the venture with the depressing tip we were about to visit – justifying, at least to myself, this otherwise mad proposition!

En route to the village, I caught a large twig under the car which then made an endless and slightly worrying noise as we drove along. We stopped and Keith got out to remove it. The lane was muddy and there was some muttering as a dark suited, black shoed partner grovelled under a spattered car trying to grasp the offending branch. Not an auspicious start! Maybe the grimy streets of London and the suburbs were preferable!

But I should not have been so faint hearted. Although we viewed the property with me resuming my endless commentary of possibilities and Keith making virtually no comment throughout, at the end of the viewing he said he thought we should look into it further. I could not have asked for more! Being the sensible businessman that he is, he suggested that we should get a structural survey done and, in the meantime, we should visit as many other village shops and do as much research as possible. This might not have been the green light but amber would do and I was off! I contacted the agent and was recommended a surveyor whom I duly appointed. He was an interesting man of ponderous nature, fashionably shabby country clothes, the inevitable four by four car and a shock of unruly golden hair.

Whilst our surveyor clambered in bird-filled lofts and lifted ancient drain covers, we started on the whole process of researching the owning and viability of village shops. In the mid 1990's there were more village shops closing than ever with the endless pressure of big supermarkets and the evolution of internet shopping. Not an obvious time to be launching into the business! We needed to be sure we had a chance of making it a success. There were a number of agencies willing to help and give advice and amongst them were The Countryside Commission and a charitable organisation called Village Retail Services Association (ViRSA). The former organisation had a retail consultant called Tony Foss working for it and Tony proved to be an invaluable friend and advisor. Tony came and looked at the existing shop and its position and gave us his realistic opinion on its future. That opinion was that it could be made to work but it would need a considerable investment both financially and in terms of effort. The latter was not a problem and the former was not an initial problem but it had its definite limits!

It was Tony who put us in touch with ViRSA and we made an appointment to go and see its founder, Derek Smith, who lived in the village of Halstock, about 10 miles away. Derek had set up this organisation as a result of Halstock's problem with its own village shop when the owner decided to sell and there was a possibility of the shop closing for good. Derek was a charming man (sadly no longer with us) who was a retired gentleman farmer living in a lovely, rambling, old sandstone manor house. He entertained us to tea in a large old conservatory housing massive grandfatherly geraniums. He was positive but searching in his questions and really made us think about what we were taking on. He challenged us but he did not dampen our enthusiasm! He offered to put us in touch with a member of the Association who ran a Post Office and convenience shop on the outskirts of Weymouth. Bill was happy to have potential shop owners spend the day with him to really see what life behind the counter was like and we jumped at the opportunity.

In the meantime, a large brown envelope arrived at our rented house at Hartley Wintney and it contained the weighty tome that was our structural survey. The list of remedial work required seemed endless but not unexpected – no damp course, re-wiring, re-plumbing, no central heating etc. etc. However, there were no major structural defects, no subsidence, the roof structure was sound, the walls were solid, in other words we had a viable proposition in terms of the property. Now all we had to decide was whether we were going to put in an offer!

Some would have called it blind optimism, others would have called it lunacy and others, including a solicitor friend who actually lived in Charlton Horethorne, said "you must be mad!". But we wanted to start a new life, we knew our financial limits and we had enormous enthusiasm so in November 1995 we put in an offer for this Cinderella of a property in the firm belief that we could uncover a Princess.

The childlike excitement and stomach churning butterflies with which we contacted the estate agent soon evaporated when our first offer was rejected and a protracted set of negotiations ensued. The estate agent informed us that there were other parties interested in the shop and cottage, at least one of whom, we later learnt, was a property developer, and that our initial offer was not acceptable. The owner was an elderly widow, Mrs. Peacock, living in Gillingham and her daughter was handling the sale on her behalf with the agent. However, the daughter lived in Australia! Offers had to be faxed and were received and despatched at hours of the day and night which suited neither party! The usual bartering process took place. Our position started at the asking price less the not inconsiderable cost of making the house liveable and the shop operational. The vendor began from the premise that the whole thing could be knocked down and redeveloped at considerable profit! Unbeknown to us, this was an option of last resort as the elderly lady who owned the property desperately wanted to preserve a shop for the village. We also later found out that two people who were to become pivotal in our early days, Pam and Colin Hilton, had exerted some friendly influence on the vendor's daughter as they had known her very well before she went to Australia. Nevertheless, several weeks of tortuous long distance bidding and counter-bidding carried on until, on Christmas Eve as we were packing up to go to Sherborne to stay with my parents, the telephone rang and the agent told us our last offer had been accepted! We bought a bottle of champagne and set off for the West Country. As we drove through the village en route for our Christmas destination we slowed down and looked at our new home with the confused emotions of achievement at having secured a deal and the gut-wrenching realisation of what we had taken on.

January 1996

Whilst lawyers earned their not insubstantial crusts corresponding with each other about the ownership of boundary walls which had been constructed with no reference to law but merely to keeping farm animals in their allotted fields, Keith and I were tackling the ever-increasing issues relating to restoring two properties and starting a new business. Someone who was to become a rock of stability in this kaleidoscope of decisions was our architect, and friend, Tim MacBean. We had chosen Tim not only because of his excellent reputation as an architect but also following an early demonstration of his dedication to his work. Having been given Tim's name and having found that his offices were within walking distance of my parents' house, we penned a note asking if we could meet him. It was the Boxing Day immediately after we had been told that our offer for the property had been accepted and we walked up to Tim's office to put our letter through his office door. To our amazement, we found Tim in the office and we spent the next half an hour or so outlining what we were planning to do. Such enthusiasm for his work had firmly convinced us that Tim was the man for us.

We had lots of ideas about what we wanted to do with the properties and Tim remained enthusiastic and optimistic even when we began to feel that the number of plates whirring about on sticks above our heads was beginning to get dangerously large. One such occasion was a January morning in 1996 when we had arranged to meet Tim at the shop with his faithful assistant, Peter, to discuss the proposed refurbishment. In recent years, we have not had much snow in the West Country but on this morning the sky resembled the ceiling of the inside of a battleship and the white flakes drifted past the window at forty five degrees like slow motion Frisbees. The glass double doors at the front of the shop did not fit too well on a good day and today the east wind blew them ajar, allowing the damp stain of melting snow to spread across the wooden floor. The compulsory buckets were in place although they were not filling too speedily as the temperature inside the shop was not too different to that on the outside. An all-pervading gloom spread through the premises as the atrium, which usually complimented the inadequate electric lighting, was coated in an opaque layer of snow.

We stood and surveyed our empire with something approaching panic as we made polite conversation to the stalwart helpers in their fingerless mittens. However, the door flew open and our cheery architect shook the snow off himself like a big, friendly Labrador and beamed a smile of greeting.

"Lovely morning! Still, never mind, doesn't look as though it will settle. You know you've got some real potential here. Now, what have you got in mind?"

The gloom lifted and we poured over drawings and sketches. Peter held a mammoth tape measure as we measured walls and established that nothing was square! Tim went out to his Land Rover and came back with a giant torch and we peered into the store at the back. There had been dire warnings of collapsing roofs and suchlike, hence the Acro props, but Tim and Peter braved the unknown and declared it entirely safe. We had considered knocking the store down if it had been confirmed as being hazardous but Tim could see no structural reason for the props being there and he recommended we take them away and use the space!

We all agreed that the atrium would have to go as it leaked like a sieve and really did nothing for the general ambience of the shop. We would fill in the hole in the roof, install a false ceiling and put in modern shop lighting. Tim agreed to get an electrician along to check out the electrics in the shop and the cottage, which we guessed could be in a fairly dire state. Keith and I needed to talk to some experts, as well as the management of the Post Office, on shop layout to get some ideas for the refit but one thing we did not want to change was the floor. Whilst it needed re-sanding and sealing, it was obvious that the wood strip floor was both original and of very good quality and it was in keeping with the image of a country store. Vinyl was not an option!

Having aired our thoughts on the shop, we went through into the cottage and gave Tim our ideas for our future home. These included an extension over the existing kitchen to give us a new third bedroom and an upstairs bathroom, taking the space occupied by the existing downstairs bathroom into the kitchen, installing French doors from the lounge to the rear patio, putting in a damp-proof course, installing central heating, re-plumbing, re-wiring, creating a utility room from the lean-to shed etc. etc. The list seemed endless. After about two hours we parted, numb with the cold and the enormity of the task. Tim went back to start drawing up a specification for putting out to tender to builders and Keith and I returned to London to try and carry on our jobs with as much enthusiasm as before. We drove across a bleak, windswept and snow-streaked Salisbury Plain and we had the first of many "board meetings" convened in the car whilst en route from one destination to another. One thing was certain, life would never be quite the same or quite so exciting.

Whilst Tim beavered away at drawings and specifications, we started to get our heads around how to stock and run a village shop. My contract with a large city insurance broker was coming to an end and, alongside finalising a new corporate grading structure, I spent several happy hours on trains commuting to London reading "how to run a village shop" books. I made notes on purchasing, mark-ups, turnover etc. etc. and at weekends Keith and I produced what we considered to be best-case and worst-case financial models. A lot of what these books contained was standard management advice that we had encompassed in our careers – but some of it was not! Like getting your stock right!

As luck would have it, about the time we were struggling with this conundrum – observation at the local supermarket only served to confuse and depress with its complexity – a shop in a village about 10 miles from Hartley Wintney was being heralded in the local press, following its successful saviour from closure. Never being afraid to explore all avenues, we found out the name of the lady who had master-minded this turnaround and we contacted her. We soon learnt that village shop owners have an instant camaraderie, akin to the resistance, and they are always willing to share advice and anecdotes if they feel this aids the crusade against supermarkets! The lady owner of the shop in question was only too willing to help and invited us to visit the shop, which we did one weekend.

We must have looked a curious sight as we toured the shop, at a snail-like pace, dictating the name of every product into a hand-held tape recorder! I then spent interminable hours at the word processor, transcribing our observations and sorting them into baking products, preserves, tinned vegetables, household goods, pet foods, stationery – the list went on and on. Having produced this weighty tome, we were totally bemused and confused as to how to turn it into a shop full of useful stock. Just because this worked in green belt Hampshire, would it work in Charlton Horethorne? And even if it did, where were we going to get it all from?

Time to talk to our font of all retail knowledge, Tony Foss. Tony listened, with the patient, indulgent air of a favourite uncle, to the confused ramblings of a couple of potential retailers and came up with the obvious solution. Were we prepared to pay for the services of a retail consultant? We had not budgeted for this but we viewed it in the same light as getting a structural survey on the property – a sensible precaution against a potential disaster. And, said Tony, the consultant could advise on the layout of the shop! The layout – another mysterious area of expertise about which we had no knowledge and, in all truth, at this stage, one to which we had given scant thought. We were more worried about what we were going to sell than what we were going to put it on! As a result of this conversation, Tony put us in touch with Robert Bacon (appropriately named) and we briefed him on what we needed from him, namely help, advice and a blueprint to work from! We left him to go and visit the shop and surrounding area and come back with his recommendations whilst we dealt with the 101 other things that seemed to be on our plate.

February 1996

One of the factors, apart from blind optimism, which persuaded us that this venture could be a success was the effort that the people living in the village had put into keeping the shop going whilst it was up for sale. A committee had been formed under the chairmanship of Jenny Vaughan-Jackson, a lady conveyancer, and it included a local land owner who was the Chairman of the Parish Council, a retired naval officer, a retired nurse and several other notable members of the village community. All these good souls were very keen to see the village retain the last of what, at one time, had been a number of shops and they, together with a large number of stalwart volunteers, had been stocking and manning the shop for nearly 18 months. The committee even dabbled with the idea of buying the shop themselves, as a type of village co-operative, but, for a number of reasons, abandoned this idea.

At our first meeting with them, over a bottle of wine one evening, the committee were both welcoming and helpful but we could detect some underlying scepticism as to whether these "townies" actually knew what they were doing or whether they would produce the sort of shop the village needed. We made it clear that we wanted to take the village with us on this project and we asked the committee's advice on how best to communicate with the residents. They told us that there was a well-read parish magazine, which was published monthly, and that we could either put articles in the magazine or we could circulate a letter, or whatever we wanted to issue, with it. Excellent – we had a channel of communication! We left the lady chairman's pretty thatched cottage feeling that we had made real progress on the communication front but, we were under no illusion, that we would be the subject of intense scrutiny and analysis after our departure!

Back in my office in London, the project I was working on was winding down and I was finding it increasingly difficult to enthusiastically present my findings on the job analysis which I had been carrying out, when I really wanted to be concentrating on the best range of soups to stock. This dual purpose in life was emphasised one morning when the phone rang in my office and a pleasant young lady asked if I was the person who, with my partner, had bought the village shop in Charlton Horethorne? When I said that I was, she introduced herself as a researcher for BBC Radio Bristol and asked if I would be prepared to do a live interview later on that morning? I said "yes" but when I put the phone down I realised what I had let myself in for.

I called Keith and told him what had happened. He was very supportive – and delighted that I was doing it and not him! We agreed the line I would take – good news, optimism, praise for the village – no downbeat angle about previous failures and political disinterest! I then called my parents and asked my father to have the tape recorder primed and ready – never had my family taken such an interest in Radio Bristol! I then waited on tenterhooks for the phone to ring – and the predicament into which I had got myself began to dawn on me.

I was sitting in an office in the City, surrounded by other employees, supposedly doing a Human Resources project, waiting to talk on live radio about buying a village shop. I dared not go and get a coffee or go to the loo in case the phone rang and I missed the call – or worse still, a colleague answered the phone and found themselves in the middle of an incomprehensible interview. What if my boss rang and called me up to his office immediately – what excuse could I give for up to an hour's delay? And even if none of these things happened, what if I was trapped into saying the wrong thing during the interview and I irrevocably upset all our future customers? By the time the call actually came I had a knotted stomach, sweaty palms and a vision of both employment and retail doom before my eyes. I need not have worried – none of my fears were realised, no-one burst in through the office door mid-interview and the questions were friendly and easy to respond to. After a tense build-up of what had seemed like hours, the whole thing was over in less than three minutes and I had a combined feeling of relief and anti-climax.

When chatting over my whole media experience that evening with Keith, we started wondering how Radio Bristol had got hold of the story. After all, we had only just bought the property, it was not as if we were already open. Some research via the village committee established that Dennis, the retired naval officer, was a very active member of the local political scene and consequently had a number of contacts in the local press. Dennis, now sadly no longer with us, had fed the story to the press of the sterling efforts put in by the community in keeping the shop open together with the news that we had bought it and planned to restore it to its former glory. Hence the call to my office and the resulting interview. Obviously the publicity was good and the motives were laudable but we did make a mental note to try and take the initiative ourselves and not be caught on the back foot again.

March 1996

It was early March when we decided to take up the offer of a visit to Weymouth and see Bill and Wendy James in operation in their shop and Post Office on the outskirts of the town. A pleasant telephone conversation with Bill augured well for a successful visit and it was agreed that Keith would take on this particular task. The morning of the appointment broke to a covering of snow but, undaunted, Keith set off with encouraging news on the weather and road conditions. All was well and Keith arrived mid-morning to a warm welcome if, perhaps, a slight tone of "do you know what you are in for?". Bill and Wendy concentrated on advising Keith on the running of the shop, rather than the Post Office, with a run-down of stock, pricing, special offers and hoped-for profit margin. Wendy was particular adept at extracting more purchases from a customer than they had intended to make when they came in and she also had useful tips on the positioning of stock to entice customers to buy. Bill and Wendy were gracious hosts, both with food at lunchtime and the imparting of their experience. Keith returned with yet more ideas, all of which made us eager to get started and put some, or all, of these thoughts into practice.

The fax and the telephone were red hot between Tim MacBean and ourselves as plans and drawings for the refurbishment of the shop and cottage took shape. We met up in Tim's office every couple of weeks and tossed ideas around and tried to cover every detail of the plans before Tim put them out to tender to a range of local builders. About this time, Keith and I decided to award ourselves a special holiday before we took on the rigours of opening a shop for 364 days a year. So at the end of term, we gathered up my son, Richard, and his friend, Lewis, from school in Taunton and took them back to our house in Hartley Wintney for the night prior to flying out to Antigua for ten days' holiday. The whole complexion of our future could have potentially changed on the evening before our flight when the four of us sat down to a Chinese take-away. We had the television on and the weekly lottery results were being announced. As the numbers were drawn we became quieter and quieter as, one by one, the first four numbers were on our ticket. Our euphoria was short-lived, however, as we had none of the remaining numbers. Hey ho – it was going to be a shopkeeper's life after all!

The hotel and facilities in Antigua were superb and whilst the boys canoed, sailed and ate their way through the holiday, Keith and I sat under a palm tree deliberating on every aspect of our new business. We gained the interest of the American owner of the hotel when Tim faxed through to the hotel sheets and sheets of builders' specifications for us to approve. We pored over them, comparing them to the drawings which, rather sadly, we had packed in our cases, while a tropical breeze wafted the papers around and we desperately tried to keep them free of drips of rum punch. To this day we still have the sheets of shell pink, Pineapple Beach Club, headed paper on which we faxed Tim our amendments and our instruction to go out to tender.

When we got home from our holiday, reality set in. Keith went back to work, the boys went back to school and I completed my contract and became a lady of leisure. Leisure! This was a word that had very little meaning for us for the next seven years. A cacophony of tasks faced us. We had to find an accountant, register for VAT, get a business bank account, acquire a machine which would allow us to take credit cards, find suppliers, agree our stock range and layout with our retail consultant, find shop fitters and shop equipment, decide on a builder, confirm with the post office our suitability and understand how that relationship would work, get an off-licence and so on and so on and so on!

Robert Bacon, our retail consultant, had completed his research and contacted us to arrange a meeting to discuss his proposals. He forwarded a weighty document to us which we devoured with eager anticipation, writing our comments and questions in the margins for discussion at the meeting. The three of us met one lunch time in the St. Ermin's Hotel in Westminster. The good news was that, despite the current climate of village shop and Post Office closures, Robert felt that the shop had every chance of success given its position, size and the positive attitude of the residents. This conclusion was also helped by the fact that we were in the fortunate position that we were moving from the highly priced properties in the south east of England to the less expensive south west. The other positive result which we could draw from Robert's proposal was that, barring some retail marketing expertise regarding the layout and product mix, he confirmed very much the conclusions we had reached whilst carrying out our own research and projections. It was comforting to know that our business expertise was proving to be transferable. The less good news, and I suppose it was to be expected, was Robert's assertion that we would need his services from now until we opened, and ideally beyond, if we were ever going to achieve our goals! We thanked him profusely, said we would think about it, paid an extortionate price for three drinks and three rounds of sandwiches and left, confident that we could manage the next stage of the process without his help.

Our next major meeting involved the opening of the tenders that Tim had received from the builders for all the work involved in refurbishing the shop and the cottage. Keith had important business meetings so I drove down to Sherborne to Tim's office for the grand letter opening ceremony. As usual, Tim hospitably offered coffee and whilst he fetched it I stared at the six unopened envelopes which contained probably the biggest work estimates either Keith or I had ever seen. With a deft movement of the letter opener, Tim slit the first envelope and our eyes shot to the bottom line figure. Oh. That was more than Tim had estimated but still, one had to be more expensive! Wrong. The remaining five were larger than the first! I got this sick, butterflies feeling in my stomach, coupled with a cross between panic and misery. How were we ever going to afford all this? I left Tim's office and rang Keith. As usual he was philosophical and calm, saying we would look at the quotes in detail when we both got home. The next weekend was spent crawling through the detail of the specification, re-examining our finances and making sure all the quotes had been made on the same basis. At the end of all this, we concluded that we could go ahead, more or less as planned, and we contacted Tim and asked him to appoint D.J. Chutter as our builder – one important decision made.

We now had a provisional start date for the building work, some time in April, and we thought it might be timely to communicate this both to the volunteer committee and the local residents. The committee had agreed to carry on running the shop until it was refurbished and we could take over, for which we were eternally grateful, and the post mistress from the neighbouring village had similarly agreed to carry on in the interim. Having told the committee of the proposed timetable, i.e. building work to start in April, refurbished shop to open in July, we sent out the first of what were to be dozens of

Newsletters over the next seven years. We introduced ourselves to our future customers and told them the broad outline of our plans – and with the help of the editor of the Parish Magazine, our missive found its way to all corners of the parish.

April 1996

Although this venture meant that we would be the masters of our own destiny, we still had one employer – the Post Office. The shop, over its long history, had had a succession of, in the early days, men and, latterly, women, as its Sub Postmaster. We had been assured, as part of the deal when we bought the shop, that the Post Office management had agreed that a Post Office would continue in the shop in Charlton Horethorne. In the mid 1990's, a Post Office was still very much an integral part of a village shop and, with benefits and pensions still being paid in cash, a Post Office guaranteed at least a minimum number of customers across the threshold. However, the downside from our point of view was that we still had an "employer" for part of the business – the very thing we had looked forward to getting away from. One of us had to be designated as the Sub Postmaster and we had decided that it should be me so, with some trepidation, I set off to Taunton to be interviewed by the Regional Network Manager, Simon. I had been given directions which, initially, lead me to the main Post Office in Taunton, then through a side door, up some stairs and into an office area. This had definitely seen better days and the grey metal desks and filing cabinets and brown lino floor gave a rather tired and depressing aura. Simon, however, was very pleasant and friendly and gave the impression of being so laid back he was almost horizontal. The "interview" turned out to be more of a three way discussion between Simon, myself and a lady colleague of his and I got the impression that, barring two heads or a criminal record the length of the Kray twins, anyone would have been acceptable for the job. After all, what other business takes on employees who are expected to provide all their own work accommodation and equipment and then stand the risk of being robbed or held at gun point, whilst being paid a very meagre salary? Not many – and we decided that it would not pay to stop and think too hard about what we were taking on.

The conversation with Simon ranged over a wide agenda of topics, some of them merely confirming what we already understood and some of them, frankly, rather astonishing. Firstly, Simon confirmed that we would be able to open the Post Office six mornings a week for which we would receive the princely sum of £7 per hour. We could open for longer hours if we wished but we would not receive any payment for the extra hours – a not entirely attractive proposition. We would receive an allowance for annual holiday – hey, holiday, there was a word we had not been contemplating – but any cover we provided would have to be someone who had previously been approved and trained by the Post Office. If we wanted to take anyone on to help on a regular basis in the Post Office, their recruitment, training and pay was down to us but we would still be deemed to be legally responsible for any work they carried out. Considering I did not have a clue how to run a Post Office at this stage, the idea of training someone else seemed akin to carrying out brain surgery – tricky to say the least! I decided to put that one on the back burner for the foreseeable future.

On the subject of training, Simon said that shortly before we re-opened, I would be required to go to the Post Office training centre just outside Bristol for a one-day familiarisation course. Then, when we re-opened, I would have a trainer with me on-site for the first two weeks, holding my hand and showing me the ropes. She would order all the stock and manuals required and train me in all aspects of the job, including the weekly balance. Weekly balance? These were two words new to my vocabulary and I enquired further. To my dismay, I learnt that, every Wednesday afternoon, I would be required to balance the business conducted the previous week with the stock on hand at the time. I asked, with growing disbelief, if this meant counting every stamp, postal order, coin and note and I was told that it did and, further more, if it did not balance, I had to find the error before the following day's business. I was then shown, to my increasing horror, two forms, the size of small tablecloths and covered in numbers, columns and the indecipherable abbreviations that every business indulges in just to prove its complexity. These were, apparently, what had to be completed weekly, in duplicate, using carbon paper. Carbon paper – we had not used that in the outside business world for 10 years. I was trying to keep all this in proportion – after all there were thousands of Post Offices all over the country and I was not aware of wide-eyed, manic Sub Postmasters running around the streets every Wednesday having been driven to distraction by the weekly balance. It surely could not be as bad as it looked!

The conversation was moving on to more material matters, like the actual layout of the Post Office itself and the screening and so on. To my amazement, Simon announced that we would be expected to re-utilise the screening which was already in the shop, subject to making it fit the agreed space. The Post Office in the existing shop had moved around a fair bit, depending on the aesthetic and business desires of the previous occupants. At present, what passed for a Post Office was located at the back of the shop and was in a decidedly scruffy and dilapidated state. The glass window, with its sliding hatch through which business was conducted, was dirty and scratched and coated in filthy grease applied by some previous Sub Postmaster who, presumably, could not get the hatch to move smoothly. The re-use of this screening was not what we had in mind as part of a modern, classy, refurbished village shop but Simon was not for moving on this point. I could see many hours of cleaning and scrubbing ahead of me if this Post Office was ever going to look presentable.

The next bombshell was the safe – or lack of one. The previous safe had been dragged, heaven knows how because it was immensely heavy, into the kitchen of the cottage when thieves thought they might be on to a good haul. Having broken into it through the side with what must have been a glorified tin-opener – no safe-breakers these – they found it had virtually nothing in it. According to the good folk who were running the shop at this stage, the thieves were so irate that all their labours had yielded nothing that they returned to the shop and threw its meagre supplies of flour and eggs everywhere, adding insult to injury for the volunteers who arrived the following morning. We had specified that, as one of the conditions of purchase, the safe be removed from the cottage before we completed on the deal and this had been done, so now were without a safe. We had naively thought that, as we were to be custodians of significant amounts of the Post Office's money and stock, they would be supplying us with a safe means (pardon the pun) of storage. Wrong again! I was astoundingly told that the provision of a safe was down to us. We were totally responsible for the safe-keeping of the Post Office's property but whether we kept it under the mattress, in a sock or in a state-of-the-art safe was our decision. I think at this stage I was speechless.

We ended on a topic which, looking back on it, would have been laughable had it not also been taken so seriously. Anyone who, as a child, played shops and Post Offices would remember the fun using the Post Office Stamp. The heavy thud somehow implied authority and power and it set the user apart from any other provider of a service to the public. It had a "don't mess with me" aura! This feeling continues into adulthood and I will confess to a sneaking tinge of anticipation at being in charge of this symbol of power. It did not take long for this enthusiasm to wane when I was shown the stamp and how it worked. I was handed two tins, one containing a pad of midnight blue ink and one containing tiny metal numbers and letters like the printing sets one had as an eight year old. I was then shown how, every day, I would have to change the date with tweezers! I enquired about the date stamps I had seen in large Post Offices – shiny and chrome, not dark grey metal with a wooden handle – and I was told we could have one of those if we wanted but we would have to pay for it – £60! I made a mental note – Keith had been wondering what to get me for my birthday!

I left Taunton with a feeling of complete confusion. I was relieved that the "interview process" had been virtually a rubber-stamping exercise and that I would, in due course, be able to get the Post Office in Charlton Horethorne up and running again. However, this was tempered with a large dose of misgiving that not only were we going to be beholden again to an employer, at least for some of our business, but also that that employer seemed to be stuck in a 1960's style of management! Still, in the scheme of things, at least that plate was still spinning!

The interior and exterior of The Village Shop in 1996

"Bramble Cottage" – or "Storr House" as it was previously known – in 1996

The jungle, otherwise called the back garden !

The original Post Office

The vandalised safe left in the cottage kitchen

The back garden emerges from the jungle

The builders take over

May 1996

Our next task was to try and find suitable suppliers for our stock. We approached this in a number of ways. We talked to the committee who had been running the shop, albeit with a minimum of stock. Their main grocery purchasing was done via the local cash and carry, Bookers in Yeovil, 10 miles away, and involved a trip once or twice a week to stock up. We made an early decision that, if it could be avoided at all, we were not going to use cash and carry as our main stockists. Not only was it not necessarily cheaper than a wholesaler who delivered, but the whole idea of buying for a shop in the same way as you would do your domestic shopping, albeit in bulk, seemed a nightmare and a total waste of our valuable time. Prior to our holiday in Antigua, we had travelled down to Exeter and visited the annual Taste of the West exhibition which introduced us to a number of West Country produce suppliers, such as Dorset Farms' ham and bacon and Dartmouth Smokehouse's smoked fish. This show also had exhibitors such as the Post Office and Camelot (the national lottery organiser) and we discussed our situation at length with them. In addition, we visited the stands displayed by Mace, Londis and Spar and this gave us an early insight into the role, and business restrictions, of what are called "symbol groups". We had already taken the decision that, if at all possible, we wanted to retain the "independent identity" of the shop and whilst there would have been major buying benefits from belonging to groups such as Mace, Londis or Spar, we did not want their names plastered all over an attractive village shop. We need not have worried – they were not interested in us! With minimal trading over the previous eighteen months and a recent tenant who had gone bankrupt, we were not deemed to have a good track record! We were on our own!

We talked to the staff manning the Camelot stand about being allocated a lottery terminal which we felt would be another attraction to customers. They informed us that, at that time, all the terminals which were going to be installed in our geographical area had been allocated – and, anyway, as we were going to have a Post Office, if we were to be allocated a terminal it would have to be via the Post Office! Here we go again – the long arm of Post Office bureaucracy strikes again! We moved over to the Post Office stand to discuss this with them and this only served to confirm what Camelot had said. Even worse, if we were to have a terminal, the Post Office took a percentage cut of the business we carried out. Ultimately we decided not to pursue this whole issue of a lottery terminal further, particularly when it became apparent that, unless you achieved a certain volume of weekly business, the terminal would be removed! We decided that it was better not to have been a lottery agent at all than to have started and then had the agency removed – not a very positive business message.

The shop committee had been providing daily newspapers and they introduced us to the cartel that is the wholesale provision of newspapers and magazines. We had been completely unaware that newspaper wholesalers basically come to an industry agreement as to which wholesaler would cover which geographical area. This resulted in a monopoly situation where retailers had no opportunity to shop around. As there seemed no point in fighting a battle which we could not win, we saved our energies for other causes and, to be fair, WH Smith, the wholesaler when we re-opened, was extremely helpful in recommending a range of magazines and other material for us to stock in the beginning.

We did, however, make a conscious decision not to stock "top shelf" magazines despite the advice that they were good sellers. This was not a decision made based on over-prudish feelings about the magazines but to save ourselves, and possibly a good proportion of our potential customers, from any unnecessary embarrassment!

Given that we had initially rejected the idea of joining a symbol group and we did not fancy the cash-and-carry route, we needed to find ourselves a local wholesaler who would deliver the bulk of our core products. Who better to ask than our guardian angel, Tony Foss, who, as usual, came up trumps and we were introduced to Wincanton Wholesale who were based less than 5 miles away. Armed with our researches and Robert Bacon's recommendations, Keith met one of the directors of Wincanton Wholesale in the skittle alley of The King's Arms, the next door pub. Not particularly auspicious surroundings but better than our newly acquired cottage which now resembled a demolition site following the arrival of the builders. After several hours of discussion and refinement, an agreed stock list was compiled and we felt much relieved that we had a local wholesaler on board who would deliver weekly and whose prices were similar to if not less than cash and carry.

We had somewhat assumed, in our ignorance, that one or two wholesalers would be all that we needed. How wrong can you be? Milk! There we were, in the middle of the Somerset countryside with, at that time, three dairy farms in the village and we did not know where we were going to get our milk from! We were recommended to a dairy called Lordswood in the village of Penselwood, about 5 miles away. They turned out to be excellent and were as local as we could achieve. Bread! The committee running the shop had persuaded a local baker, Roger Oxford, to supply them with bread and Roger very kindly agreed to continue supplying us, as well as providing us with freshly baked cakes. Fruit and vegetables! My mother regularly used a greengrocer in Sherborne and she mentioned to the owners that we were looking for a supplier. Sue and Ted Watts could not have been more helpful and not only advised us on what to stock but agreed to supply us from what they bought for their own shop and deliver it three times a week. We were making progress! We still had to source frozen food and stationery but at least we were now ticking items off our list, not just adding to them!

Whilst all this was going on, the cottage, which was going to be our home in due course, was being demolished. We only came down to Somerset to view progress, or the lack of it, every two or three weeks – it was all we could cope with. Under pain of death, the builders were told that they must preserve, at all costs, the beautiful walnut staircase which, to be honest, was the best bit of the house. They took us at our word and encased the handrail and banister in old carpet whilst they ripped out electrics, plumbing, bathroom fittings, kitchen units and old doors, stripped off plaster, took down walls, took up floors and generally took the whole property back to its shell. We had planned to extend the cottage over the existing kitchen area to allow us to move the bathroom upstairs. However, on one visit, we were greeted by Tim and the site foreman, Dave King, with prolonged sucking through teeth. We learnt during this project that, the longer the sucking through teeth, the greater the cost would be! Dave was a taciturn man in his fifties with greying hair and beard who, with his permanent, leathery tan, could have passed for a Greek fisherman. Dave was a real craftsman when it came to building anything with stone and, as a foreman, he commanded the men's respect – no-one was allowed to sit in Dave's chair when it came to tea breaks.

The reason for the gloom and despondency on Tim and Dave's faces was that, despite previous optimism, they now both felt that it would be impossible to build on top of the existing kitchen structure. It was just not strong enough. We would have to demolish the existing kitchen and outhouse (otherwise known as the utility room) and start from scratch. More expense. In our heart of hearts I do not think that we were totally surprised but it was an additional cost that we could have done without. We had no option but to give them the go-ahead because without moving the bathroom upstairs the kitchen would be very small and without extending upstairs we would lose a bedroom and so on and so on! We tried to be philosophical. Keith was still working in London, my contract had been terminated early so I had negotiated some severance pay – and hopefully the shop was going to make money. We would manage somehow.

The demolition of the existing kitchen yielded two surprises. The first was an interesting piece of structural engineering. The current kitchen was an extension built at right angles onto the back of the original cottage. Obviously a doorway had had to be knocked through from the cottage to the kitchen and, quite correctly, a rolled steel joist had been put in over the opening to support the wall above. So far so good! Anecdotal information had indicated that the previous owner of the house, Mr. Peacock, was tall, about six foot five inches, Keith's height, and obviously low doors would be a problem to him. When the kitchen was demolished and the RSJ was exposed, it looked as if some giant, metal-eating caterpillar had attacked it! Presumably to raise the head-room in the doorway, the RSJ had been cut away in a general arch shape, resulting in only about 4 cms of metal remaining over the centre of the door. It was on those 4 cms that the wall above rested. The builders hastily installed Acro props to shore up the wall until a new joist could be installed.

The second surprise was much more exciting. Having demolished the kitchen, the builders started to dig new footings for the foundations of the new extension and they unearthed a Victorian bottle dump. Every colour of glass emerged from the hole, most of it broken but the occasional complete bottle was found. One of the builders, John Starks, lived in the village and he came to know that I was interested in what was being excavated. If he found any whole bottles, he would carefully put them on a wall in the garden for me and each time that we visited the site I would collect any specimens he had found. I ended up with about ten bottles of different shapes and sizes and I still have them on display in the kitchen now.

There was another distraction as far as the builders were concerned during this project. She was young, attractive and French! Tim MacBean had friends in France whose daughter was in England as part of her university course to become an architect. As she needed to complete some time on a practical building project, Tim asked if she could spend a couple of weeks with Chutters' team working on our refurbishment. We happily agreed – until we saw her! We threatened to bill Tim for the loss of building productivity as the Chutters' men fell over themselves to help her!

With Keith still working in London and the cottage like a bomb site, we used to come down every second or third weekend to meet Tim or see suppliers or whatever needed doing and we stayed with my parents in Sherborne. It was frustrating not being able to do anything in the house or shop yet but we could start to tackle the garden. We are both keen gardeners and we were looking forward to turning this long, narrow patch into a traditional cottage garden. The first job was to clear the ground and this bald statement belies the work involved. The garden was totally overgrown with nettles, brambles and ivy and there were a number of self-sown elder trees. One weekend, Keith, my son, Richard, and I set about hacking our way from one end of the garden to another. Apart from ending up with four, two-metre high piles of debris to be burnt, the biggest surprise was the size of the garden when we had cleared it – it was half as wide again as we had thought it was. We had also fully revealed the beautiful view from the bottom of the garden out across a pretty, secluded, curved valley where our neighbour's cattle grazed and where, on a fine evening, the sun set casting a stunning golden glow on the sides of the hills.

Our neighbour on one side was a dairy farmer whose main yard ran alongside our dividing wall and garage. Jim's parents had farmed the land before him and, on one occasion, when leaning over the wall for a chat and an inspection of our progress, Jim declared that the land on which our garage and drive stood had been sold by his father to Mr. Peacock many years ago. He also added, rather dourly, that no doubt his father had sold it for a pittance – and, of course, it would be worth a lot more now!

The opposite side of the garden from the farmyard bordered the neighbouring pub garden. The dividing wall was in a pretty poor state and, because of the lie of the land, it was possible to stand in the pub garden and look straight into our plot. The landlords of the pub at that time were a couple called Dot and Neil Stedall. Dot was a vivacious, chatty person but her husband, Neil, was a slightly downbeat person whose life was always half empty, not half full. One weekend we were working in the garden, still trying to dig out nettles and dandelions when Neil appeared over the wall.

"You'll never get anything to grow in there. I've been trying for years", he said.

We were not going to be put off by such pessimism and made some "Oh well, we'll give it a try" type comments. About this time, we were bracing ourselves to broach a couple of tricky issues with Neil. We were about to start the process of applying for an off-licence so that we could sell alcohol and we knew that, currently, the locals went into the pub if they wanted to buy a bottle of wine or some cans of beer to drink at home. We also planned to sell cigarettes and, again, we knew the current source of supply was the pub. We were nervous of the landlord's reaction when he realised he could be losing some of his trade. We did not want to get off on the wrong foot with our neighbour. We need not have worried.

"I suppose you are going to apply for an off-licence?"

"Yes, that was the plan."

"Oh, brilliant, that will stop all those people coming in at the weekend just for a bottle of wine!"

"And are you planning to stock cigarettes?"

"Yes."

"Good, I won't have to mess about with that cigarette machine and give out change any more!"

Mission accomplished! A happy landlord and two happy future shopkeepers, although we were still rather astonished by Neil's totally laid-back attitude to losing a tranche of his business.

One of the major tasks we had to complete was obtaining an off-licence for the shop so that we could sell the alcohol we had bragged about stocking to Neil. Not having a clue as to how to go about this, we spoke to our local solicitor who had handled the purchase of the property and it transpired that the firm had an expert whose sole role in life was to handle licence applications. David was a grey-haired man, not far off retirement, who took his job very seriously and whose office was stacked from floor to ceiling with the copious paperwork involved in this process. We completed the necessary documents and David informed us that we would have to appear in the Magistrates Court to explain the rationale for the application and convince the Court that we were suitable applicants to be granted the licence. The due date arrived for our Court appearance and we arrived to be met by David. We waited to be called alongside various other attendees, most of whom were appearing for a variety of criminal infringements. We sat nervously, dressed in our best business attire, grasping various files and documents containing information about which we thought we might be asked.

Finally, we were called and we stood side by side in the dock feeling more like criminals than licence applicants. We were then interrogated, by the Magistrates, about our suitability to hold a licence and our knowledge of selling alcohol, for what seemed like hours, although it was probably only about fifteen minutes. We felt we were eminently suitable applicants but we had to admit that our knowledge base was a bit slim – we were more used to buying booze than selling it! The local police confirmed that they had no objection to a licence being granted and, as a consequence of this and, presumably, our reasonably convincing performance, we were granted a provisional licence, subject to Keith attending a one-day training course.

When we came out of Court, feeling a little battered but somewhat relieved, we asked David what was meant by a provisional licence. He told us that, as we were refurbishing the shop and the actual placement of the off-licence section, as we had shown it on the plans we had submitted with the application, was yet to be built, the Magistrates would only grant a provisional licence. Once the shelving was in place, the Magistrates would carry out a site visit and, subject to that being approved, we would have to appear in Court again for the full licence to be approved. This came as a bit of a blow to us as we had thought we were going to complete the process that day. Nevertheless, we had at least started the ball rolling and we would just have to hope that we could get everything completed by the time we re-opened the shop.

In between what were diminishing insurance tasks, Keith went into the office each day with lists of people to ring, letters to draft and documents to read. For instance, we had brochures from all the main banks giving details of their business accounts. After much deliberation and reading of small print, we settled on Lloyds and opened an account in Yeovil. The manager in charge of business accounts was John and he became a valuable ally in the first few months of business. Our larger suppliers wanted reassurance that we would be able to pay their bills and John's help in this was tremendous. Until we started trading we had no financial credibility, but we could not start trading without stock and John's ability to convince our suppliers of our credit-worthiness was invaluable.

Keith's background in insurance gave us a head start in choosing an insurer and in Richard Wood, at the NFU, we again found a friend. Richard thought nothing of calling in on his way home with any documentation or information we might need. A great help when trips to his office would have interrupted important things like shelf-stacking.

To complete the trio of necessary but not very exciting specialisations, we chose Ian Dodd as our accountant. Ian was the partner in a firm of accountants in Sherborne and what could be better than putting a Scotsman in charge of your finances? He provided excellent advice on how to set up our accounts, how to optimise our tax position and how to register for VAT. Getting all these specialists and their services lined up was vital for the smooth running of the business even if it was not as attractive as tasting a new brand of smoked salmon!

When it came to how customers might pay for their goods there was always cash or, with our newly opened bank account, cheques but a modern business was expected to be able to take credit and debit cards. Keith again ploughed through the various companies' promotional literature and eventually settled on Barclaycard. It came as quite a surprise to us the level of charges imposed by the various credit card companies – Barclaycard was 1.4% – and there was another initial problem. The credit card swipe machine worked via the telephone line and it could not be activated until the line was in place and fully operational. At the time when we were selecting Barclaycard we had no idea when our telephone lines would be connected or what the numbers would be. To see us through the early stages of trading we were given what became known as the "whizzy machine"! This was the old-fashioned desk-top device into which you inserted the customer's card and a multi-part document and then slid a bar across the top to get a card imprint on the slip. To say that this was temperamental would be an understatement – a blurred imprint, torn or puckered slip, a slip inserted upside down – you name it, the possibilities were endless. We were very pleased when we finally had our telephone link installed, although that was not without its problems. More about that later!

We still had two substantial gaps in our list of suppliers, namely frozen food and stationery. Having asked the oracle, Tony Foss, he told us that a company called Snow King would be the most suitable for frozen food. We contacted them and they were very helpful, not only recommending a stock list but also promising to come and actually stock our freezer immediately prior to opening.

The committee in the shop had been buying a minimal amount of stationery from a wholesaler called Hobbs in Blandford Forum. We went down to visit them to discuss our needs and we walked into a warehouse like Aladdin's cave. Not only did Hobbs sell every conceivable item of stationery but they sold toys, greetings cards, wrapping paper, maps, party tableware, balloons and banners. We were like children in a sweet shop! We met one of the directors of the company and a charming man called Robin Cuff and between us we managed to produce a list of the stationery items which we collectively thought would sell. Once again, Robin offered to come and put all our stock on shelves, hooks and in card racks for us prior to opening. Wonderful!

Having made real progress on the supplier front, we now had to concentrate on the layout of the shop and employing the services of a shop fitter to fit it out for us. Robert Bacon had recommended a layout for the shop which, with some modification, we were generally pleased with. He had talked me out of my initial idea of having a small coffee shop in one corner. He said that we needed to maximise the return per square foot – technical-speak for the fact that we had to sell as much as we could from the floor space we had – and a coffee shop was a poor use of the space in financial terms. As it turned out, he was right but on two counts. The financial rationale was no doubt sound but the idea that we would have had time to serve teas and coffees on top of the work involved in running the shop and Post Office was, in retrospect, laughable.

Robert had also given us the name of a shop fitter, County Shop-fitting, based in Portsmouth, who not only came highly recommended but was also approved by the Post Office when it came to fitting out our new Post Office area. We contacted the owner, Quentin, and arranged to meet him at his offices. He was a delightful man who ran his business with his son and one or two staff and he went through our plans and drawings with us in great detail. Quentin was not at all surprised that the Post Office had specified that the old partitioning had to be reused. This was apparently standard practice and he was used to having to make do and mend. He said he would draw up detailed plans and submit them to the Post Office for approval so that he was ready to proceed when our builders had done the basic refurbishment of the shop. We also talked to him about chill cabinets and freezers and we ordered an upright cold drinks cabinet, a chilled food cabinet and a chest freezer from him. The shop currently had a small freezer and a fridge which we planned to put in the back store to take any overflow stock.

Since our initial "hello" newsletter, we had not put out any further communications to our future customers and we thought it was time we rectified this. For some time we had been chewing over the idea of putting out some form of questionnaire to establish what the village was looking for from its shop. After many hours of tossing around possible questions, we drew up a comprehensive questionnaire to send out to the village. We covered everything from opening hours to product mix, from possible services we could offer to preferred newspapers and magazines. Having put a lot of work into drawing this up, we wanted to ensure that we got the maximum response and we agreed with the editor of the parish magazine that we could distribute it via the magazine again. To optimise the response, we included stamped addressed envelopes with the questionnaires and, as a gesture of our gratitude, we also made a donation to the parish magazine. All this was time-consuming and fairly costly – although considerably cheaper than employing a consultant to do it for us! We also felt that it was an important exercise to carry out, not only as a source of information for ourselves but also to identify to our future customers that we cared what they thought. Anyway, it could all be an academic exercise if no-one responded!

We left a pile of questionnaires and envelopes for distribution on one of our weekend trips to Charlton Horethorne. As the magazine was only published monthly, there was inevitably a time delay before we got any response and the wait was agonising. Then, one morning, two or three recognisable envelopes arrived with the post in Hartley Wintney and I tore them open in excitement – our first response. I could not wait for Keith to come home that evening to show him. In the next couple of weeks the replies flooded in and eventually, when the flood dried to a trickle, we had received a response of over 75%. We were delighted. I then spent each day collating the replies and analysing the response. The results were helpful and, in some cases, informative and certainly gave us food for thought. In particular, we had listed a number of services we could provide and the most popular proved to be photocopying, faxing, dry cleaning and the supply of Calor Gas cylinders. The former two would be relatively easy to provide as they were facilities we anticipated having for the business anyway but the latter two would require a bit more research.

June 1996

Building work was carrying on at a pace although everywhere still seemed to look like a bomb site. We had regular meetings with our builder, Dave Chutter, and his son, Mark. Dave was a short, stocky man with a round rubicund face, glasses and a twinkling smile. He was a carpenter by trade but had built up a successful general building business and he commanded the respect, and not a little fear, of the men who worked for him. By this stage, we were beginning to try and tie Dave down to a completion date for the shop and for at least part of the cottage. We were resigned to the fact that we would be living in some discomfort for a while but our main priority was the completion of the shop so that we could open and start trading.

With the agreement of the volunteer committee, the usable area of the shop had been reduced by half and a plastic sheeting screen had been erected so that work could be carried out at the rear of the shop. This involved partitioning off an area which we would use as a dry store and as an office area housing the safe, photocopier, fax and word processor. We were also having a sink, toilet and washbasin installed and the back store, which, when we bought the shop, was being held up with Acro props, was fitted out with shelves together with a back door being knocked through so that we had rear access from the cottage garden. All this had been achievable whilst keeping the shop operational but the time was approaching when this would no longer be feasible. The leaking glass atrium had to be removed, the roof re-felted, a false ceiling and lighting had to be fitted, the floor had to be sanded and resealed, the shop front had to be replaced and so on and so on. There was also an ancient wooden loft ladder which accessed the large loft area at the front of the shop and which, inexplicably, came down and blocked the main shop doors when it was extended. This had to be removed and a new, modern loft ladder had to be installed in a less obtrusive position. It was obvious that the shop could not remain open whilst all this was carried out but equally we did not want the village to be without its shop.

We searched around for a solution and came up with the idea of hiring a portakabin in which to house the shop for the interim. We found a company who could hire us a suitable unit and we then had to talk to the Highways Agency about positioning it on the road outside the shop. They were not keen. However, undaunted, we proposed knocking down the wall which bordered the cottage front garden – it needed rebuilding anyway – and putting the portakabin on the front garden. This meant that there was minimal intrusion onto the lane and the Highways Agency agreed to our proposal. Having sorted out the logistics, we approached the committee with some trepidation as we were not too sure how they would react to yet another test of their endurance. We need not have worried. In their now familiar stoical fashion, the committee readily agreed to move out into the portakabin, with the proviso that we helped with the physical move. We were only too pleased to agree. In some respects I think the volunteers were glad to get away from the incessant noise of drilling, sawing and hammering coming from behind the temporary partition.

Time was marching on and, at the end of May, Keith retired from his job in London. This was a time of immense anticipation and excitement but it was also tinged with sadness as Keith left a company and colleagues with whom he had been for over thirty years. We had a weekend away in the New Forest and then it was back to Hartley Wintney to carry on planning our future. Our house in Hartley Wintney was a furnished, rented house and we already had furniture in store from the Camberley house which we had sold previously. We knew the cottage would not be finished by July, the planned opening date for the shop, so we had to contemplate putting more of our belongings in store and only keeping out those things which we would need for the first few weeks. We had been promised a bedroom, shower room and a rudimentary kitchen so we set about making lists – yet more lists – of belongings to go into store, belongings to be put somewhere in the cottage and belongings to keep with us whilst we stayed with my parents for the first couple of weeks of life in the South West. It was a nightmare! The man from the removal company, which was already storing some of our things, looked completely bemused by the complexity of our domestic arrangements

After much pressurising and intransigence, we managed to convince our builder that the shop would be completed by the beginning of July. When we told Mark Chutter that we intended to start living in the cottage around then, the colour drained from his face. Sadly, Dave Chutter had suffered a heart attack during the course of the project – he later assured us that we were not the cause – and whilst he was recovering, he had handed over the reins to Mark. After much sucking through teeth, Mark agreed that our bedroom would be complete and we would have a basin and toilet but that would be all. We also agreed that the removal men could leave our belongings in the shop, covered with dust sheets, until that space was needed, as the cottage was in no fit state to have anything left in it.

Even the promise of our bedroom being ready seemed a slim one. Upstairs you could look from one end of the cottage to the other with nothing but vertical wooden supports for the currently absent walls to the rooms. There were also some strategically placed Acro props to one side of our bedroom which were the result of a panic telephone call we had received from Tim one day. As well as having the L-shaped kitchen extension built on the back of the original cottage, at ground floor level an eight foot wide single storey extension had been built right across the back of the house. This had formed a rear link with the shop, with a door directly into the shop and a corridor across the back of the house to the downstairs bathroom. At that time, these were the only toilet facilities available to anyone working in the shop. We had decided to block off the door leading into the shop, put French windows out onto the garden and convert this area into a study. Not only was this a better use of the space but it stopped direct access from the house to the shop. This seemed a good idea to us as it both divorced "home" from "business" and it improved security.

The flat roof of this extension ran the length of our bedroom, which had been partially extended over this space, leaving the remaining area as a balcony accessed by French doors from our bedroom. This balcony had two French doors leading onto it, which we thought was excessive, and we were having one converted into an ordinary window with a window-seat. It was during the course of this work, and the replacement of the ceiling, that a serious problem was encountered. The usual A-frame timbers of a roof structure, by definition, rest on the tops of the walls for their main support. Not in this case. When the plaster was stripped back and the ceiling removed, the builders found that when our bedroom had been extended over the downstairs study area, the wall had been moved outwards and the A-frame of the roof was resting on – nothing! Hence the panic telephone call and the Acro props. More expense, another rolled steel joist, but at least we could sleep easily knowing that the roof would not fall down.

With our worldly goods shortly to arrive as well as stock due before too long, we had to get our security system installed as soon as we could. A local company called South West Security had been on the recommended suppliers list provided by the police and they had proposed the level of security, alarms, panic buttons etc. that they thought we would require. As usual, the Post Office had an input into the subject and had to approve the proposal. Included in their requirements were two foot-operated panic alarms under the Post Office and shop counters. These, together with the personal attack buttons we had fitted in the house, would automatically alert the security company's control centre which would, in turn, alert the police. A comforting precaution, if rather disconcerting.

Because the system covered both the shop and the cottage, and was operated via a telephone line, we had the fatal flaw that it could not be activated until the telephone lines were installed, which could not be done in the cottage until the building work was at an appropriate stage. It was at this time that we decided to move into the cottage as soon as practicable so that we could be on site to protect our property.

Just before we left our house in Hartley Wintney, we received a letter which made us doubly sure that we had made the right decision about our future. Each year, in June, the village held its Feast Day, similar to a village fete, and the letter was from that year's Feast Day Chairman, Gary Rendall, asking if I would formally open the 1996 Feast Day. Opening fetes was a new experience for me but, as village duties went, it was distinctly preferable to judging people's pets or children. Hopefully I would not make too many enemies this way. On the day, the whole task was not too onerous and it gave me a chance to publicly thank the volunteers for continuing to keep the shop going in the portakabin and also to apologise for any inconvenience caused to the village. This included, as we had heard on one of our visits, our builders cutting through the main cable of the village's electricity supply and plunging the whole village into darkness. There were advantages at times to being over 100 miles away. Feast Day was fun in the true village sense of stalls, parading majorettes, cream teas in the village hall and guess the weight of the piglet! I do not think the piglet was actually the prize but we did not win so we will never know. We felt very welcome and we could not wait to move in

One of the many things that had taxed us was what we were going to call the shop. At the time we opened we were not married and, whilst Fortnum and Mason and Marks and Spencer have a certain ring about them, we did not feel that Browning and Gudgeon had quite the same cache. The name of the village, Charlton Horethorne, is long enough in its own right without trying to incorporate it into a shop name. We had a dislike for the word "Store" or "Stores" as it had either American or warehouse connotations. So after much brain-storming we came up with the obvious – call it what it was – "The Village Shop". And so we now had to find ourselves a sign writer who would turn our vision into reality. A quick scrutiny of the local yellow pages found us the name of Phil Rushworth and he joined our ever-increasing army of suppliers, helpers and advisors.

Phil was a talented artisan who drew up a proposed name board for the shop which, because of its size, would have to be made in three pieces and then installed once the builders had finished painting the front of the shop. The outside of the shop and cottage were to be painted a pale cream and we chose burgundy and dove grey as our theme colours for our signage. We wanted to have a notice board to put in the window to carry adverts and village notices and Phil also made this for us to match our main sign. There was only one problem with this notice board. Phil had made it so substantially that it weighed a ton. We used it all through our ownership of the shop but many was the time Phil's name was taken in vain! The other item that Phil made for us was an A-board with "The Village Shop, Open" on it. This board had a horizontal piece of wood at the top, joining the two vertical pieces, and this in turn had a large circular hole in it. This made it look like a rather strange commode! Phil's idea was that we could put a pot plant in the top to make it more decorative. The theory was fine but, as with all Phil's work, the board was substantial and extremely heavy. We started to use it but, as this meant lifting it in and out four times a day, Keith abandoned the whole thing in favour of his health.

As part of our preparations for opening, we produced a leaflet giving our opening times and the range of products and services we would be offering. Again, we had thought long and hard about our opening times and we had to reach a conclusion based on gut feeling as there really was not any custom and practice to build on. We were not going to employ any staff to start with because we wanted to learn the business fully ourselves first and also we had no idea whether we would be able to afford to employ anyone. We therefore tried to devise an opening pattern which would serve the needs of our customers without us killing ourselves in the process. We settled on opening at 7.30 a.m., closing at 1.30 p.m., re-opening at 3.00 p.m. and closing at 6.30 p.m. during the week. We were working on the continental principle of a lunchtime/siesta closing period and we would re-open in time to benefit from any trade resulting from parents collecting their children from the primary school. We also felt that we needed a break after doing 7 hours work before we carried on and did another 3 hours in the afternoon. The weekends were different, with a planned opening as usual on Saturday at 7.30 a.m. but closing at 1.00 p.m. We would then re-open for 2 hours at 5.00 p.m. to try and catch the "I've forgotten the bottle of wine" trade. Sunday would be a 9.00 a.m. opening with a closing time of 12.30 p.m. These hours were considerably longer than the village had been used to for a number of years and we hoped that they would be happy with the arrangement – and that we could survive it.

We had arranged to rent a photocopier and we already had a fax machine so we were sorted as far as providing these services were concerned. We went and talked to the owner of the best dry cleaning business in Sherborne and came to an agreement with him that he would collect and deliver any dry cleaning from us, twice weekly. He would pay us a commission and the customers would only pay what they would have done had they taken their cleaning into Sherborne. A very satisfactory arrangement.

We had also located a supplier of Calor Gas cylinders in Yeovil. Charlton Horethorne only has mains electricity as its piped energy supply and therefore people used oil or bottled gas to supplement their heating and cooking. The provision of gas cylinders was therefore another valuable service we could supply. However, as we were going to have to store the cylinders in the back garden, and this was still very much the builders' domain, we postponed entering into an arrangement with Calor until the house was completed. It also seemed reasonable to put this on the back burner, so to speak, as we were experiencing a warm, dry summer.

Having finalised our opening hours and organised all our initial suppliers and services, we had our leaflet printed. When the box arrived, with our smart grey and burgundy pamphlets, we were thrilled and excited and we really began to feel that this was all actually going to happen. As part of our publicity surrounding our opening, we decided that we should deliver our new leaflets door to door, as well as having them available to hand out in the shop when we opened. We not only hand-delivered these in the immediate village but we went to surrounding villages and hamlets that did not have shops such as North Cheriton, Poyntington, Stowell, Sigwells, Blackford and Milborne Wick. Not only did this educate us in the geography of the area but we also received a higher education in the idiosyncrasies of people's letter boxes!

I spent one day at the Post Office Training Centre in Bristol, which really did not increase my overall knowledge greatly. The main benefit was meeting other new Sub-Postmasters and hearing how they had come to find themselves in the same situation as us. Their circumstances varied but some seemed more attuned to what they were going to be facing than others. One couple ended the day looking like startled rabbits caught in the headlights. Probably because we had so much else to try and organise, any concern I had about how I was going to run the Post Office just became another item on the list of things to get to grips with.

By this stage the shop was really taking shape. The new shop front, incorporating two display bays and two integral flower planters, was finished and the false ceiling and new lighting had been installed – a dramatic improvement. The most significant and amazing improvement however was the shop floor. Although it was blackened and dull, it was a wooden strip floor that Tim thought was probably oak. We decided that we wanted to retain it, as a wooden floor was in keeping with the type of modern but rustic décor we wanted to achieve. Although we were not around at the time, we were told by the volunteers that it took several days of sanding to restore the wood to its former glory and the workmen doing it looked as though they had been in a Sahara sandstorm. Once the wood had been stripped back it was then sealed and it looked magnificent – more like a deep, honey-coloured ballroom than a shop. It was then covered by yards of plastic sheeting whilst the decorating was carried out and until the shop-fitting started to ensure that it looked as good as possible when we opened.

Prior to Opening

Finally, our moving day arrived and we were up at the crack of dawn packing the last of our clothes and folding bedding. The removal men worked all morning getting our worldly possessions into the lorry and we crammed the car with all the things which we thought were too precious to entrust to them. By about 11.30 a.m., we had cleared the house and we set off for Charlton Horethorne. The removal men had said that they would be stopping for an hour en route for lunch and, given that the lorry was not the fastest vehicle on the road, we soon had quite a head-start on it. So, we decided to stop at a pub in Winterbourne Stoke for some lunch and to recover after the morning's efforts. We were sat in the window of the pub, finishing whatever it was and chips, when, to our horror, we saw our removal lorry going past! We dashed to the bar to pay and fled back to the car. I am not sure whether the landlord thought we were some fugitives on the run but we must have looked highly suspicious. We managed to catch and overtake the lorry and arrive in Charlton Horethorne about 20 minutes before it did.

The painters were still decorating the inside of the shop but they had cleared a large space in the middle of the floor for the removal men to use. The lorry driver and his mates looked pretty shell-shocked when they saw the state of the house we were moving to – with its temporary shop in the front garden. They dutifully unloaded our worldly goods into the shop and piled them on the floor like a shipment from Oxfam. The pile was then covered with dust sheets and the process of moving us from Hartley Wintney was complete. With heartfelt wishes of good luck and an air of total disbelief, the removal men bade us farewell and said they looked forward to bringing our stored furniture down to us before too long. With equally heartfelt conviction, we said so did we!

Apart from finally getting down to the West Country, the major benefit of moving was being on site to pressurise the builders into making the house habitable for us and into completing the shop. We were now in June and we needed to have a bedroom which was fit for occupation, a room in which to store our belongings so that we could clear the shop for the shop fitters and some plumbing that worked. We eventually got to the position where our bedroom was usable, no refinements but usable. It had been decorated and the builders put some curtain rails up for us but there were no wardrobes and the floor was bare. This was not as bad as it sounded because the floor had actually been rather nice polished wood – I say "had" because it had suffered the ravages of building work. Nevertheless we cleaned it up as best we could and the builders helped us get our bed and a sofa bed up to the room. The former was obviously to sleep on and the latter was to sit on and eat or watch TV. I think the builders realised that it would have benefited them as well as us if they had got our room finished by the time the removal men had arrived. Getting a king sized double bed and an iron-framed sofa bed up a set of narrow, twisting cottage stairs resulted in some very red and dripping faces and a fair amount of colloquial local language!

The front spare bedroom contained our boxes of pots, crockery, cutlery etc. from our previous kitchen and we set up what would ultimately be a pine bedroom work top for Richard's bedroom as a kitchen workbench. This housed a box of groceries and our microwave. All this was necessary because of several major problems. Firstly, the kitchen and new extension were nowhere near finished – in fact that end of the house was only partly built and was open to the elements. Secondly, we had no running water or toilet facilities in the cottage, only the sink and toilet in the back of the shop. Thirdly, the electrics in the house were minimal to say the least. In order for us to move in, the electrician provided us with enough electricity to give us lights and use either the microwave or the TV but not both at the same time. Despite all this we decided that, after a couple of weeks of comfort and pampering with my parents, we were going to move in. We wanted to keep the pressure on the builders and we were also concerned about the security of our personal possessions and our stock, once it started to arrive.

Luckily the weather was warm and dry but our first night in the cottage was pretty basic. We forgot, not for the last time, about not switching on the microwave and the TV at the same time and we heard what became a familiar clunk as the fuse tripped. Keith became very practiced at grabbing the torch and picking his way down the stairs and along planks balanced on breeze blocks – the hall floor was still up whilst new drainage was laid – to reset the fuse box. We were also apprehensive about being joined by a variety of wild life as there was still no back on the house – luckily this did not happen, or at least we were not aware of it. Our other problem was the lack of bathroom facilities. Why is it, when normally you do not need to use the toilet during the night, knowing that to get there will involve crossing a back garden resembling an assault course, your bladder gives you twinges which you spend all night trying to ignore? Well, ignore them we did and we saved ourselves not only the balancing act in the hall but picking our way through trenches in the garden before we could make it to the relative civilisation of the shop.

With the builders' help, we moved our remaining pile of belongings from the shop into the two downstairs reception rooms in the cottage and cleared the space for the shopfitters to start. At this time, the safe was also delivered and we had to be absolutely certain as to where we wanted it positioned as it was extremely heavy and it would not be possible to move it if we got it wrong. The day that Quentin and his team arrived, we began to get really excited. As piles of shelving, wall board, brackets, units, counter tops and racking poured off the van, we could really begin to believe that our drawings and plans were coming to life. Keith and I had spent hours cleaning the old Post Office partitioning and it now looked passable if not exactly smart. We were slightly alarmed to see a large sheet of steel being concealed in the front of the Post Office counter and even more so when Quentin said that it was to avoid us being shot in the legs during a raid! Not very comforting but a sensible precaution, I suppose!

Gradually, as the days wore on, our shop came to life and, in order to maintain the element of surprise, we covered the shop windows to minimise prying eyes. Nevertheless, visitors to the portakabin shop could not resist a peep in the door and there were regular "ooh's" and "aah's" heard as they took in what they saw. Once all the shelving, counter and units had been installed, the chill units and freezer arrived and were switched on ready for their contents. We had, by this stage, settled on an opening date of 13th July and we had set up all our suppliers to deliver at times to meet that date. Obviously, things like stationery and groceries could be delivered before perishable products like chilled food and greengrocery and some items like milk and papers would only arrive on the day we opened. However, whilst there was still some finishing work going on which was causing dust, we did not want anything delivered too soon.

One area of the business which was still not finalised was the off-licence which would enable us to sell alcohol. With the work on the shop virtually complete, we asked our solicitor, David, to arrange the Magistrates' on-site visit with enough time for us to appear in court again prior to us opening. As part of our first order with Wincanton Wholesale, we had ordered our wines, beers and spirits and it would be a pity if we were not able to sell them. One afternoon we were standing outside the shop as suppliers came and went and wearily carried boxes back and forth when a lady and a gentleman, in the casual, tweedy clothes of the retired country landowner, came up to us and said "hello" and did we remember them? We confessed that we did not and they introduced themselves as two members of the Magistrates bench. We changed in an instant from tired, grubby shop owners who were somewhat irritated by this further intrusion on our time into two people trying to portray professional dynamism with a finger on every business pulse. In any event, having taken in the layout of the shop, the Magistrates seemed pleased with what they saw and said that they would report back positively. We rang David straight away and he said he would get us in to the next Magistrates' sitting. Great, we thought, virtually home and dry. It will just be a formality when we go back to court. Little did we know!

We presented ourselves, as before, at court, feeling quite relaxed on this our second visit. We could not have been more wrong. The Magistrates sitting that day were different from the previous hearing and they proceeded to give us a sustained grilling. You would have thought that we were possibly the last people on God's earth who should have been permitted to sell alcohol. We kept our nerve, however, and left the court feeling battered and bruised but the proud possessors of an off-licence. We would not, after all, have to consume all that stock ourselves although, the way we felt that afternoon, we could have made a serious dent in it anyhow!

The reign of the resilient volunteer committee was coming to an end and we agreed with them that we would take on any stock they had left. It was necessary, therefore, to list and value all the stock in the portakabin and we undertook to carry this out. Now what better job could there be for three teenage boys? Friends of ours, Chris and Sally Waite, had two sons, Simon and Tom, who, with my son, Richard, were commissioned to do this stock take. It was a long, laborious job which tested both their patience and mental arithmetic. They then spent many warm trips carrying piles of stock from the portakabin into the shop. Sally, however, came to the rescue of all of us by arriving at lunchtime with a superb picnic which we consumed sitting on the village green.

The stock we inherited was an interesting collection of groceries, confectionery and miscellaneous "useful items". Amongst these were some extremely ancient light bulbs and some vintage cards of fuse wire, apparently dating back to Mr. and Mrs. Peacock's day when they stocked everything from tractor parts to groceries and Wellington boots. We displayed the fuse wire and similar items for a few weeks after we opened but, finding no enthusiasm from our customers for such pieces of retailing history, we eventually consigned them to the bin.

A very useful inheritance from the volunteer committee was their system of newspaper folders. We had taken the decision very early on that we would not deliver newspapers to people's homes. There were two reasons for this. Firstly, in a rural location with houses scattered down unlit lanes and sometimes down fairly long drives or tracks, it would have been a nightmare to try and organise a newspaper round. It would not have been feasible, or even safe on dark winter mornings, to have young newspaper boys or girls carrying out deliveries. And we would certainly not have the time or the inclination to do it ourselves. Secondly, we worked on the principle that if people had to come to the shop to get their papers there was a very good chance that they would buy something else.

The newspaper folder system was simplicity itself. Each customer who requested a daily or weekly newspaper or magazine was given a folder with their name on, details of their order and how they wished to pay. As and when their order came in, be it daily, weekly or monthly, their publication was put in their folder and their folder was left out on display for them to collect when they came in. This ensured that everyone received what they had requested and that they could collect it at their convenience. After seven years of running the shop, we could find no better method of servicing people's newspaper and magazine requirements and, in fact, our successors have carried on the same system. It also had the enormous advantage for us, when we started, of helping to put names to faces. A terrific benefit when everyone knows your name and you know no-one's.

Stock was now arriving every day and there were times when the shop resembled a warehouse. All our major suppliers were true to their word and organised the stocking of the shelves. Robin Cuff, accompanied by a young lady colleague, spent two days unpacking, pricing and displaying our stock of stationery. It soon began to look very impressive and we were like children in our excitement over packs of rubber bands, rows of neatly arranged greetings cards and brightly colour wrapping paper draped over shiny chrome arms.

We had purchased, in preparation for this exercise and for our on-going needs, four pricing guns which were now in constant use. It remained a mystery to us, and our eventual staff, in all the years that we owned the shop why, in these days of high technology, the pricing gun had to be such a pain in the neck. You could be merrily clicking away, dispensing neatly printed price labels, when, all of a sudden, the gun would decide to print over the divide between two labels rather than tidily in the middle of the label. No amount of tweaking of screws or adjusting of knobs would persuade it to do otherwise. So, you abandoned that gun and picked up another one. Somebody else then picked up the first gun.

"It's not working", you would say.

"Yes it is", they responded. "It's fine".

We swore that they had minds of their own.

The least favourite job was installing a new roll of labels. You would find that an empty gun was surreptitiously swapped for a full one so that the user could avoid the frustrating and rarely successful job of changing the roll. In future years, when large orders came in and we and our staff were all involved in pricing, there would always be an undignified rush to grab the gun with the most labels, leaving the unlucky last person with the certainty of changing the roll.

The incessant clicking of price guns was a feature of the days leading up to our opening. We were allocated a rep by our frozen food supplier and he came on the day our order arrived to load the freezer for us in an attractive and appealing way. He was a pleasant man but he bore the appearance more of a wheeling-dealing car salesman than a frozen food rep. He was tall, in his late fifties and had his greying hair, with a hint of blonde colouring, slicked back over his head. He wore sharp suits, bright shirts and ties and had a comprehensive selection of heavy gold jewellery on his fingers and around his wrist. He also wore a gold chain and medallion around his neck and he had an aura of nose-tingling after-shave. This appearance took a bit of a battering, however, after he had spent a day, head down, filling our large chest freezer with, amongst other things, fish fingers, chips, peas and Yorkshire puddings. Our rep had also acquired an ice cream freezer for us which came free and gratis as long as we had photographs of Walls ice cream all over the outside. Having fought the good fight with our main freezer, the rep then spent the remainder of the day stocking the ice cream freezer for us.

One lesson we learnt very quickly is that pricing labels do not stick to frozen food. Our rep had laboriously priced every item with what were advertised as freezer price labels, before stacking them in the freezer. However, within weeks the bottoms of the freezers were full of damp, illegible, homeless labels and our stock was un-priced. We consequently produced full price lists for our frozen products, which were displayed by the cabinets, and we abandoned the dreaded pricing gun, at least for that type of product.

The most significant amount of shelf-filling and pricing was done with our very helpful associates from Wincanton Wholesale. An enormous lorry arrived and parked outside the shop and disgorged what seemed to be an endless stream of boxes and packages. Tins, bottles, packets, rolls, bags, cans – the range seemed infinite – where was it all going to go? Well, the first lesson we learnt was not to start unpacking stuff willy-nilly. We were shown how best to categorise things – tinned soup next to tinned vegetables next to tinned fruit and so on – and that we should put some of each category on each shelf, one under another. It has apparently been shown that we automatically scan shelves vertically rather than horizontally when we are looking for something. Clever these retail specialists! We were then shown that, having decided on the category layout, we should not just start loading the shelves with, say, all our cans of soup. Oh, no! We had to take one of each flavour and lay them out on the shelves to make sure they fitted and looked right. If they did not, it was far easier to move, say, fifteen cans of soup than fifteen times twelve, which would have been the whole stock. More tricks of the trade!

Having begun our apprenticeship on shelf-stacking, we worked alongside our Wincanton Wholesale colleagues, taking surplus stock into the back store, moving goods when they thought they were in the wrong place and dealing with the ever-increasing pile of packaging debris. This was another area that we had not been quite prepared for – the mountain of rubbish created each week and how dirty it would be. Most things came either in large cardboard boxes or on cardboard trays encased in plastic. These had all previously been kept in a warehouse before being delivered to us and the plastic built up static electricity which attracted the dirt. We found our hands and clothes were getting filthy and we seemed to be permanently washing our hands.

Disposal of all this rubbish was also an issue. Whilst the village had recycling bins for glass and paper, cardboard was strictly prohibited and we made a mental note to see if we could find some way of recycling this in the future. In the meantime, we had to use the local authority refuse service to dispose of everything but even this was not as easy as it sounds. We contacted our local district council and asked for their assistance. Needless to say, we had to complete a form identifying the type of waste we wished to dispose of and we were told that they would only take away our trade rubbish in trade rubbish bags. Fine, we said, where do we get them from? You buy them from us, they said, for £32 a bundle. Game, set and match to the local authority! However, we could not really complain because South Somerset District Council had devised a scheme whereby village shops could apply for 50% rate relief from council tax as an incentive to keep the dwindling number of village shops open. This was subsequently increased to 100% relief in 2000. We had applied for this zero rating and been granted it so I suppose paying for our refuse bags was the least we could do.

The stocking of the shop was now going at a cracking pace and lorries and vans seemed to be arriving every day, much to the intrigue of all the village residents. One of the areas that taxed us at the beginning of this was how to set our prices? We were used to being bombarded on television with tales of cost-cutting and price sensitive products and we were nervous of setting our prices either so that we deterred custom or we made no profit at all. All the books that we had read and the advice that we had taken indicated that the overall profit margin for a village shop's business should be around 20%. This overall figure varies greatly between products with some, like cigarettes, as low as 5% and others, like greetings cards, as high as 100%. In terms of how we were going to set our prices when we started, we need not have worried as the vast majority of our suppliers gave us recommended retail prices for all the products they supplied. We only started to deviate from these and devise our own pricing strategy as we got more familiar with the business and, even then, we did not make any major overall changes.

Whilst the shop was filling up nicely, the Post Office did not really appear ready for business. There was no residue of stock, manuals, money or anything else in the Post Office because it had been run on a locum basis, by a neighbouring Sub Postmistress, who brought everything with her when she came twice a week. Various boxes of terrifying looking forms and leaflets had arrived together with some manuals, a book to put the stamps in and two sets of scales. Other boxes arrived towards the end of the week which I did not have time to open but as I had been told that Mary, my trainer, would set me up on the Monday, as well as organise the stock I would need, I decided to leave well alone.

Work was progressing slowly but surely in the house and we were beginning to see the fruits of our labours at the bottom of the garden. We had had a tree surgeon in to remove the self-sown elder trees and tidy up the remaining trees in the garden, including a very tall eucalyptus. As we began to walk around the village and get used to our surroundings, we noticed that a disproportionately large number of gardens contained eucalyptus trees. We could only conclude that either Mr. Peacock had done a good deal on a job lot of saplings or that someone in the village had Australian connections.

Despite its terribly overgrown state when we started work on it, we found that when we finally got down to the soil in the garden, it was excellent. It was dark and crumbly and looked as though it would be very productive so we dug a vegetable plot at the bottom of the garden, as far away as possible from the builders' work area which now sported a portaloo in a fetching shade of bright blue. We planted carrots, peas and beans and transplanted a small and sad looking gooseberry bush which we had found lurking in the undergrowth. All seemed to flourish and this gave us hope that, when we finally dispensed with the services of our builders, we could turn this into a pretty cottage garden.

In between supervising suppliers – or rather, acting as their navvies – we were trying to select all our fixtures and fittings for the cottage so that our builder could not say that he was waiting for a decision from us. We had a kitchen to organise, the fittings for a bathroom, shower room and cloakroom to choose, curtain rails to buy, light fittings to select and carpets and curtains to arrange – the list, and cost, seemed never-ending. And just when we thought we at least knew the entirety of what was needed, our builder asked what door and window furniture we wanted – knobs and catches to you and me. We did not manage to choose all this before we opened and we had to dash off during our precious lunch breaks to decide on such exciting but vital items as taps. We never knew that there were so many sizes, shapes, colours and prices of taps.

The weekend came before we were due to open on the Monday and we had transferred all the stock from the portakabin, so the temporary shop finally closed. Two of the people who had been heavily involved in the volunteer group, brother and sister Colin and Pam Hilton, very kindly offered to sort out newspapers for us over that weekend. We had communicated our plans to the village and everyone seemed quite content that we would only be selling papers in the shop for a couple of days prior to it fully re-opening on the Monday. Colin and Pam had been providing a Sunday newspaper delivery service for the village and they were happy to continue doing this when we took over. This round had come about when the voluntary committee had learnt that the existing deliverer was giving up. As part of the committee's policy of trying to keep the shop viable whilst it was up for sale, they decided to take on the Sunday paper round. This was our only concession to doing a newspaper round and Colin and Pam had become experts in the idiosyncrasies of everyone's letter boxes and the friendliness, or otherwise, of the local dog population. Ultimately, when Colin reached retirement age, he and Pam gave up our Sunday deliveries and, in the absence of any other volunteers, we changed the arrangement on a Sunday so that customers had to collect their papers in the same way as they did on any other day.

It was a wonderful relief to see the portakabin being finally removed from what had been our front garden. It marked the end of a fairly expensive exercise for us and it suddenly released a flood of light into the cottage. The portakabin had been positioned so close to the cottage that it had blocked out all the light to the ground floor at the front. We now had space, light, the full use of our front door – and a wreck of a front garden.

The weather had remained thankfully dry and warm throughout this lead-up period which had meant minimal mess from suppliers unloading their goods into the shop. To protect our newly refurbished floor during this process, we had left the plastic sheeting on the floor and this proved to be a sensible move for another reason. There were, at that time, two hunt kennels in the village, a pack of Basset hounds which, relatively unsuccessfully I think, used to hunt hares and the main Blackmore Vale and Sparkford Hunt, which had its kennels and stables behind the Manor House, on the opposite side of the road to the shop. One afternoon, just before we opened, we had the front door of the shop open to let in some air whilst we worked and all of a sudden an enormous hound from the Hunt kennels trotted in. Now I like dogs but these hounds are large and grizzled-looking from action in the field and I did not quite know how to approach it as it nosed around towards the back of the shop. Keith, not being a great dog fan, kept his distance. In one sense I should not have worried because, having found itself amongst shelving units and boxes at the back of the shop, it became quite disorientated and frightened. The downside of this was, as I shoo-ed it towards the front of the shop and out the door, it peed all the way! Thank goodness for the plastic sheeting.

The Opening

We went to bed on the Sunday night apprehensive but excited and hoping to goodness that all the money we had invested in the premises and the stock was going to pay off. We had also had balloons and pens printed with "The Village Shop" name and telephone number and we planned to hand these out to all our new customers. We just hoped that we had some! On 13th July we were up about 5.30 a.m. and made our usual pilgrimage to the back of the shop, me to wash my hair and myself, Keith to wash and shave. We had finally got a toilet in the house but there were still no washing facilities. We had breakfast and made our way into the shop just after 6.30 a.m. and we were shortly joined by Colin and Pam who had offered to help us with the newspapers. We were mightily relieved to see a large pile of papers on the forecourt outside the shop together with the milk we had ordered from Lordswood Dairy in nearby Penselwood. Ted Watts then arrived with our first delivery of fruit and vegetables and, whilst Pam and Keith worked through the intricacies of the day's newspaper orders, Colin and I priced up the fruit and veg and stacked the trays on the display. Around 7.00 a.m. we had our first customers – some builders on their way to work – and we were in business. From then on we had a steady stream of people on their way to work, followed by the village school children who were delighted to see our extensive rage of sweets and chocolates. We had also bought penny sweets for the children. We had fizzy cola bottles, jelly spiders and many others which were sweet, sugary, garish colours and thoroughly unhealthy! These proved to be a great hit and there was soon a gaggle of children waiting outside for the school bus, comparing their purchases. To our surprise, one or two adults also self-consciously bought bags full declaring that they were re-living their misspent childhoods.

Around 8.00 a.m. my Post Office trainer, Mary, arrived. Mary was a short, friendly, rotund and smartly dressed ex-Sub Postmistress who now carried out training of raw and nervous new recruits like me. She was shortly followed by a Post Office auditor. When a new Post Office opens, and they virtually classed this as a new Post Office given its recent history, all the stock and money has to be checked and signed off before the day's business begins. I was quite happy to leave Mary and the auditor to carry this out while I helped Keith with what was becoming a continuous stream of customers.

Eventually, when the Post Office was signed off, Mary called me over and there then started a very wearing twelve days of training. We unpacked all the remaining boxes of stationery and so on that had arrived and Mary stacked all the drawers and shelves in the way a Post Office should be organised. We then fiddled with the dreaded date-stamp – my swanky automatic one which I had ordered had not arrived – and set the correct date. I then stamped my first Post Office document with my Post Office stamp. Well, actually, it was just a blank sheet of paper for me to practice on , but it felt good. Then my first customer arrived. Dorothy Read was the youngest of three elderly sisters who had been born and bred in the village. Their father had worked for over forty years at the Blackmore Vale and Sparkford Hunt kennels and the three daughters all lived in the village. When we arrived in Charlton Horethorne, Trixie and Dorothy were both widows who had no children and they lived in separate cottages on either side of Cowpath Lane, facing the church. Trixie shared her life with her elderly pet goose, Lucy, and Dorothy lived with her elder spinster sister, Alice, and a flock of Bantam hens. Dorothy had come for her and her sisters' pensions – and I have never felt quite so fingers and thumbs as I did on that occasion but, with Mary's reassurance and my customer's kindly forbearance, she finally received her pensions.

The rest of the morning was spent in a state of high nervous tension whilst I tried to introduce myself to my very patient and friendly customers and at the same time attempted to listen to Mary and avoid making too may catastrophic errors. All this while the till was ringing merrily and Keith and Pam were serving the ever-increasing number of customers. From what I could hear, in between my Post Office tasks, all the comments were favourable in respect of what we had done with the shop and the atmosphere was extremely warm and welcoming.

Having, more by luck than judgement, completed my first morning as Sub Postmaster in Charlton Horethorne, the Post Office closed at 1.00 p.m. Mary then lead me through a confusing procedure of form filling, stock checking and document despatch which I thought I would never grasp, despite her assurances to the contrary. We closed on our first morning at 1.30 p.m., tired, happy and a bit bewildered. We had nowhere to go and sit to have our lunch, so we grabbed some of the pre-packed sandwiches which we were stocking and Keith, Mary and I went and sat on the bench on the village green opposite the shop and ate our lunch. I had stupidly thought that a morning of Post Office trading and induction would suffice and that, after our alfresco lunch, Mary would wave us a fond farewell until the following day. No such luck! When we reopened at 3.00 p.m., Mary took me through more essential Post Office duties such as renewal of TV licences, colour and black and white – did anyone still have a black and white TV? – sending mail to far flung parts of the globe and deciding whether it should go surface, air mail, letter post, small package, parcel post or swiftair and whether it contained a banned substance such as seeds, honey etc. etc. etc.! My head was spinning by the time she left just before 5.00 p.m. and we still had an hour and a half's work to do in the shop. This whole training process continued for the next two weeks, six days a week, and I have to confess that there were times during that period when, after Mary had gone, I was reduced to tears by the sheer breadth of knowledge I was supposed to absorb.

Despite my problems grappling with the bureaucracy of the Post Office we successfully completed our first week running our own shop. Although the first few days and weeks as new shopkeepers are a bit of a blur now, I do recall that, before we opened, we had more or less decided on who was going to be responsible for which tasks. Keith would look after newspaper and magazine ordering and returns, wines and spirits and tobacco products, VAT and all matters financial, including book-keeping, accounts and banking. I was going to take care of general stock ordering, the Post Office, fruit and vegetables and overall cleaning of the shop. As the days turned into weeks, we found that this split worked very well in practice, with the inevitable blurring at the edges. What also became apparent, though, was that the beginning of the day was one of the most intense periods of activity. So much so that, after about an hour, we had barely spoken to each other as we had been so pre-occupied with our chores. There were papers to unbundle and sort, fruit and vegetables to be checked over and brought out onto the rack, milk to be carried in and stacked in the chiller, dates on perishable goods to be checked and, one of my least favourite jobs, the shop floor to be swept. I once tried to calculate how many miles of floor I had swept in seven years but the answer was so appalling that I decided I would rather not know! I often joked that, when we finally left the shop, I would have the broom framed and hung over the mantelpiece! Overall we had had no major problems, we had exceeded our most optimistic financial projection and apart from having appallingly aching feet, we were very happy in our new-found lifestyle. Our first day completed as convenience store retailers was crowned by the cracking of a bottle of champagne which we consumed in our "bed-sitting-room" in our building-site of a cottage.

We had managed to hit our target of opening the shop in July and our next goal was the completion of the renovation of the cottage and the return to a normal lifestyle. Work was progressing but, as usual, not as fast as we would have liked but gradually things began to take shape. The first day the shower worked in our en suite shower room was one day which was momentous. Having begun our retail careers having to wash in the sink, or dash down to Sherborne with our towels under our arms for a quick bath, we could not wait to have proper washing facilities. The day the plumber announced that the shower was working was the day we felt like we had won the lottery. We closed the shop and rushed into the cottage to jump straight into the shower. I do not think two ducks in a summer shower of rain could have been any happier!

The new kitchen and bedroom extension were nearing completion and we were finally secure from the outside world – we had things like walls, windows and doors. We had chosen a farmhouse style range of units for the kitchen and, needless to say, they were not complete when they arrived. After several attempts at delivering the wrong additional doors, the correct ones arrived and the job was finished. We were told that it was not worth the supplier's time to take back the wrongly delivered doors so we passed on to our eventual successors two perfectly good but useless kitchen unit doors!

Plumbers, electricians, painters, wardrobe fitters and security system installers beavered around and fell over each other whilst they attempted to complete their various tasks. One particularly difficult job proved to be the installation of the plaster coving we had asked for in the lounge and the dining room. The walls in an eighteenth century cottage are not exactly square and we had a particularly curvaceous set in the dining room. This caused a typically British meeting of workmen, about five in all, all of whom had different solutions to the problem of fitting straight coving to a curved wall. I am not sure how they decided to resolve the issue but suffice it to say we had coving in our dining room which appeared to fit perfectly.

The installers of the security system were now in a position to complete the work involved in linking the shop and the cottage. One of their initial recommendations was that we should be on the Red Alert system because of the financial risk in the shop and particularly the Post Office. This system allowed us to trigger the alarm directly to the police if, heaven forbid, we should be faced with a gun-toting villain, without the main audible alarm going off. This was deemed to have two advantages. Firstly, the would-be robber would not be aware that the police had been alerted and therefore there was more chance of an arrest and secondly, we were advised that an audible alarm could trigger a violent response from the intruder and we were safer having an inaudible system.

We were happy to go along with this advice, if only for the sake of self-preservation, and therefore the system was geared up in this way when the wiring was completed in the shop. It had, however, occurred to us that if one of us was on our own in the shop and such an event took place, the person in the cottage would not know there was a problem until the police arrived. The security company came up with a solution which was a 4 cm red light on the wall in the corner of the hall which would flash when the alarm was triggered in the shop and alert whoever was in the house to the problem. Fine, we thought, so this light was duly fitted ready for the activation of the security system in the cottage and the decorators carefully painted around it when they decorated the hall. However, when it came to the commissioning of the complete shop and cottage security system, the security company announced that they had found out that the Red Alert system was not available in Charlton Horethorne and we would have to have the audible alarm system after all. What about the red light, we asked? Well, they said, you will not be needing that now! So, to this day, there is a red light installed in the hall of the cottage which, no doubt, will remain a mystery to successive owners and possibly the source of much speculation!

Excitement was beginning to mount. It was now October and we had fixed a date for carpets to be laid, curtains to be hung and furniture to be delivered from store. We could not believe that we were finally going to get our home back. The first noticeable difference when the carpets were laid, apart from the sense of unaccustomed luxury, was how much quieter it was everywhere. It was not just the muffling of sound that you get from carpet but also the number of builders in and out of the house reduced drastically – taking your boots on and off is such a chore!

The day the removal lorry arrived from Guildford with the last of our worldly possessions was a wonderful day. Pam and Colin Hilton came in to help us keep the shop running and, once the Post Office closed at 1.00 p.m., I was able to enjoy the job of placing our furniture with Keith and the removal men. The men who delivered the load were the same team who had moved us down in June and they were pretty impressed by the changes they found. They even purchased their lunch from the shop which endeared them to us even further! We had bought a new three piece suite and we managed to co-ordinate the delivery of that with the remainder of our furniture so that night in October 1996 we sat for the first time in our lounge, in front of our fire, having eaten our meal in our farmhouse kitchen and we really felt that our dream had finally come true.

A Victorian bottle dump unearthed in the cottage garden

Sue and Keith's bedroom ceiling with a totally unsupported beam

Sue opening the 1996 Feast Day watched by Pam Hilton and the Feast Day Chairman, Gary Rendell

The "temporary shop" in the Portakabin outside the cottage

Signwriter, Phil Rushworth, putting up the new shop sign

Dan Hutchings and Sue stocking the refurbished shop

*Sue and Keith's bedroom and temporary "kitchen"
– otherwise known as "the middle-aged squat" – in July 1996*

Village Involvement
– Or How We Never Said No!

We gradually settled into a business and domestic routine, getting used to early opening, afternoon snoozes, long days and incessant product ordering, shelf stacking and cleaning. We also started to get to know our customers better and as they came to know us we began to get more involved in village activities. The first of these activities was totally virgin territory to us and the approach came from a most unlikely quarter. The farmer next door to us employed a herdsman named Fred Paulley, a man in his fifties who, given the nature of his job, was always dressed in grimy trousers and waterproof jackets and caked Wellington boots. Fred was a frequent visitor to the shop during the day and one day during our first September in the shop, he came in and asked Keith a most unexpected question.

"Would you like to come to a pantomime casting meeting this week? We have a very active pantomime group in the village and we are always short of men!"

Keith was somewhat taken aback because performing in a pantomime, at this stage, was about as far removed from his unfulfilled ambitions as flying to the moon. There was also a slight air of desperation in the comment "…we are always short of men"! However, not wishing to offend our new customers and being slightly curious as to what this would involve, Keith agreed to go to the meeting and later that week, giving up precious evening relaxation time, he set off to the village primary school.

Towards the end of the evening Keith returned and to my question of "How did it go?", he replied "I'm not sure!" Apparently all had started well with the assembled throng being given pantomime scripts by a lady director who, incidentally, did not live in the village but had been imported by someone who had declared her to be "an expert director with a lot of previous experience". Different people were allotted different parts to read and the reading began. All went quite happily until the last part had been read. Then, however, the session fell to pieces. The lady director started to cast the pantomime and all hell broke loose. At least two people stated that unless they were given specific parts, i.e. those other than the ones they had been allocated, they refused to take part and when the director indicated that she would not be changing her mind, these would-be pantomime stars stormed out of the school hall ! There then developed further, but less dramatic, dissent from other members of the cast and the meeting broke up in disarray! From the sidelines, we took this as a salutary lesson that newcomers should not lay down the law when they did not know the personalities and inter-relationships involved and we awaited developments with interest.

For about a month the proposed annual village pantomime was in total jeopardy but finally the "expert director" was despatched and the regular participants in the pantomime got together and settled their differences. The production was back on track and Fred asked Keith to play an emperor which he agreed to with some trepidation as he had never before trodden the boards. Rehearsals began in October and I joined the backstage crew helping paint scenery which I thoroughly enjoyed. I had always been keen on drawing and painting but this new task was on a scale which I had never attempted before. To provide the backdrop for the various scenes in the pantomime, we painted backcloths which were huge, canvas-like curtains which could be drawn to one side when another vista had to be revealed. Painting room scenes or towns or woodlands or ships, or whatever was required, to scale, with perspective on a two metre by four metre sheet laid flat on the floor was a challenge. It was also a revelation when it was finally hung vertically and the full, hopefully convincing, effect became apparent.

This started our involvement in the Charlton Horethorne Amateur Pantomime Society (CHAPS) which continues to this day. In fact, so immersed have we become in this annual village event that in 2000 I wrote a pantomime loosely based on the adventures of Beatrix Potter's "Peter Rabbit" which was staged in 2004 and which I directed. The shop also played, and still plays, a pivotal role as the pantomime box office. This can have its moments when, in amongst grocery orders, deliveries and shop customers, you are trying to sort out two tickets for the Friday evening performance, a family party needing tickets for the Saturday matinee – how many adults and children constitute a family ticket? – and three tickets for Saturday evening being exchanged for Thursday! There were also cast members who would float into the shop and ask us to keep eight tickets for their friends, some of whom would pay on the door, some of whom would come into the shop and pay and some of whom the cast member was paying for! Fred would also pop in to announce that he had offered complimentary tickets to various members of the local press as an incentive to get them to come along and write, hopefully, a positive review of the performance. "Just leave them on the door", he would say. "They will tell you who they are when they arrive!"

We soon learnt that Fred was a man with two distinct roles in life, the herdsman and the performer. Fred had been the founder of CHAPS in 1986 and, had life dealt him a different hand, he would have made his living in the world of theatre. Whilst Fred's daytime job was often cold and dirty and played havoc with his rheumatism, put Fred on a stage and he took on a totally new persona. Fred's forte was playing the dame in pantomime and the annual search in the charity shops for oversize bras and frilly knickers became a regular ritual. Fred's enthusiasm and drive were infectious and the Society missed these when he decided to retire to the south coast in 2006. He was, however, made Life President of the Society and still travels up to see the productions that he was so instrumental in setting the standards for.

Whilst winter activities in the village are spearheaded by the pantomime, a significant event in the summer calendar is the village Gardening Club show. Keith and I are both keen gardeners and we relished turning our blank canvas of a cottage garden into an attractive and productive plot. Our interest in gardening soon became known and in early summer 1997, we were canvassed by a number of gardening club committee members to enter as many exhibits as possible in the show. This was our first experience of a village gardening show and we were somewhat taken aback by the printed schedule which we received detailing the various classes and the specifications we had to abide by in our exhibits. Length of stems, number of leaves, quantity of vegetables, size of vegetables – all were laid out. Now when you think of entering a number of those tasty carrots you have previously been pulling for your meals, it never occurs to you that they must all be identical size and shape with tops cut to match. After you have pulled thirty odd carrots and only matched four of them and you still have to find another one to make up the set, it suddenly dawns that you are either going to have to make a gallon of carrot soup or eat carrots with every meal for the next two weeks!

Despite these problems, we decided to enter a selection of our vegetables and flowers in the show and, having opened the shop and done all the early Saturday morning chores associated with this, I set off down to the village hall with our various exhibits rolling around in a basket. I mentioned that we were entering some of our flowers and here we entered another minefield. You have to provide your own vases and I toddled off with a miscellany of small glass receptacles. First problem, three stems of a particular flower, as specified in the schedule, lollop in a very undignified manner when just plonked in a vase. How was it that all the other exhibits looked as though they had been starched? I then realised that there were tricks of the trade such as stuffing your vase with florist's foam or glass beads, neither of which I had got. Oh well, make a note for next year!

Obviously you cannot walk through the village with vases full of water but I had not thought ahead and brought a watering can down with me, like all the other exhibitors! So I sneaked off into the village hall kitchen and pinched a milk jug and, rather unprofessionally, topped up my vases! I walked back up to the shop rather despondently but Keith cheered me up by saying that at least we had made the effort and the village would see that we were keen to get involved. That afternoon, after the obligatory snooze and with the shop not opening until 5.00 p.m., we strolled back down to the village hall to see how our exhibits had fared and generally view the whole show. Naturally, you automatically head to your own exhibits to see how you have done before perusing the rest – a bit like picking up you school exam results. "First", "Second", "First", "First" – we could not believe it. Just about all our produce had achieved either a first or second in its class! As we walked around, somewhat bemused, people congratulated us, patted us on the back and said "I don't know where you find the time!" We mumbled something about gardening being our relaxation etc. etc. and felt that very British sense of embarrassment at our significant success. We went and bought our cups of tea and biscuits and waited for the prize giving. To our absolute amazement, not only had we won a wide range of first and second prizes but we won the Banksian Medal awarded by the Royal Horticultural Society for the highest number of first and second prizes in the show. This can only be awarded once to any particular individual and we had managed it at our first village gardening show!

To say that we were delighted was an understatement. Keith went back up to the shop to open up for the evening session whilst I dismantled our exhibits and drained away the tepid water in my vases. That evening we sat in our kitchen examining our various certificates surrounded by snapped carrots, warm tomatoes and droopy flowers and toasted our first public horticultural achievement. We have participated in the show every year since then, with varying degrees of success, but nothing will surpass the feeling that first year.

Some of our most frequent customers were the children of the village, who ranged in age from toddlers to teenagers. They would come in with parents or grandparents if they were under school age or on their way to school, on their way home or at the weekends if they were older. Having got to know and like the vast majority of them, Keith was very interested when he was approached in 1997 by the then Chair of Governors at the village primary school about becoming a school governor. The approach, however, had a slight sting in the tail. Richard Warren, the current Chair, was planning to retire from the role in approximately two years time and he was looking for a replacement. If Keith was interested, he would take him onto the Governing Body with a view to grooming him as his replacement. Keith, by nature, does not rush impetuously into things and he was also conscious of not treading on the toes of other long-serving governors, particularly Stephen Hall and Simon Purcell, both of whom had become friends of ours. Keith decided to go along to a meeting to see what he thought of proceedings and whether he felt it was something in which he wanted to become involved.

The short version of this is 'yes' he was interested and 'yes' he was prepared to be groomed to take over from Richard as no-one else wished to take it on. The longer version is that Keith joined the Governing Body in 1997 and took over from Richard in 1999, remaining as Chair of Governors until 2007. During this period of tenure, Keith oversaw two successful OFSTED inspections, dealt with the tragic circumstances of the head teacher's husband's sudden death and its aftermath, guided the school through very tricky financial waters, attended innumerable governors' meetings, external advisory meetings, school fetes, carol services, Christmas nativity plays and sports days, cut grass, pruned trees, cleared drains and mopped up floods, sat through staff interviews, disciplinary meetings and appraisal meetings and wrote reports to parents, negotiated school leases and oversaw a variety of building projects. The upside of all this work was the continued close liaison with village parents and children, outside the confines of the shop, and the feeling that he was contributing to the continuation of a school which had been in existence for over 150 years. The downside was the unbelievable mountain of paperwork that Keith received (we had one filing cabinet dedicated to school documents), the demands on his time considering the role of governor, let alone Chair, is a totally voluntary one and the frustrations of what seemed to be a total imbalance between responsibility and authority. This was not helped by the fact that all the staff at the school lived outside the village and therefore their ability to contribute to village life was very limited. Hence the focus of any local comments regarding the school and its activities was directed towards the Chair of Governors. Sometimes all this on top of working seven days a week was quite a strain but the balancing factor was the feeling that Keith got that he was contributing to a vital and longstanding part of the overall village community.

Another, even earlier, part of the village community was its church, St. Peter and St. Paul, whose origins date from the 12th century. Inevitably, a number of people required entry to the church from time to time, apart from when there were services. Flower arrangers, volunteer cleaners, practicing bell ringers and interested visitors all wanted to gain access and it was necessary to have a central point from which the church key could be collected. Not long after we opened the shop, one of the church wardens, Jenny Hunt, asked if we would be prepared to hold the key and, when we agreed, she presented us with the most amazing, heavy, ornate key measuring about 18 cms long. From then on, and for the whole tenure of our ownership of the shop, we held the key and loaned it out as required. Our most tricky moments were when complete strangers turned up asking if we knew who held the key as they wished to go into the church, usually to carry out family history research. We always felt slightly uneasy handing it over to people we knew nothing about and used to glean as much information about the enquirer as possible. It was always a relief when they returned with the key some time later and, thankfully, to our knowledge, no problems ever resulted from this arrangement.

When we first arrived in the village, communication was predominantly carried out in two forms, a fairly basic parish magazine and gossip! The former, under the editorship of Bill Closs, a retired college lecturer, has now become a much used and prized monthly document giving all the detail of the many activities going on in the village. The latter still, needless to say, goes on and, during our seven years in the shop, we were able to watch, on many occasions, the life cycle of a story from its initial truth to its ultimate, predominantly fictional, form! To bridge the gap between these two communication formats, we developed two media whilst we owned the shop. Firstly, as I mentioned earlier, we had a very substantial, in all senses, notice-board which was widely used by local residents. We carried adverts for items for sale, local services and businesses, for which we charged the magnificent sum of 20p per week. These became a source of much interest to customers and passers-by and there were regular gaggles of people reading the board whilst out on their Sunday afternoon walks. We also put up notices for village events and fund raising activities for which we made no charge. It was noticeable, after a fairly short space of time, that not only did attendance at these events increase but also the number of events multiplied, merely because there was an easy way of publicising them locally.

Secondly, and more parochially, we had started sending out Village Shop Newsletters even before we had opened because we felt it was very important from a business and a personal point of view to communicate regularly with our customers. Over the years we sent out dozens of these Newsletters, either publicising something new in the shop or an enhanced service being offered by the Post Office or some event that we were planning to which our customers were invited. We soon learnt that our customers looked forward to hearing what was happening in what they felt was their Village Shop and this translated itself into increased customer loyalty.

Another area of village involvement was a much more informal one and that was being the central lost property office for the village. This role included looking after school bags left outside the shop by some school child who was so busy talking when she got on the school bus that she left them behind; being handed a golf ball by a customer who had found it in one of the lanes whilst she was out for a walk and she thought someone might be looking for it; inheriting numerous walking sticks and umbrellas which were left in the shop umbrella stand and which, apparently, were never missed by their owners; getting telephone calls to say there were sheep out on the road and could we telephone their owners to tell them; having strangers draw up outside the shop with a village dog on board which they had found wandering the lanes and which we had to identify and attempt to repatriate with its owners – the list was endless and quite often verging on the bizarre.

One of the more unusual requests we responded to was the urgent telephone call one morning from the step-mother of a teenager in the village. She and the father of the young man had left that morning for work assuming that the teenager was still in bed and would be rising shortly to go to school. However, at 9.00 a.m. she had had a telephone call from the boy's school to say that he had not arrived and that as he was due to sit a GCSE exam at 9.30 a.m. they were getting rather worried about his absence. Having got no reply from the telephone at the house, our customer rang us to say could we possibly go up to their home and knock on the door and find out what had happened? Keith left immediately but returned ten minutes late saying there was no reply and he rang the boy's step-mother to ask what she wanted him to do next. However, by the time we called back, the lady concerned had heard from the school who said the young man had arrived and was now ensconced in his exam. Apparently he had made his way to school in plenty of time but had only presented himself to the staff immediately before his exam was due to begin. He was not the most popular person when he got home that evening but, if my memory serves me right, he did at least do reasonably well in his exam! He is now a serving member of Her Majesty's army and, hopefully, his communication skills are much improved!

Part of our role as one of the focal points of the village included contributing to the various groups which operated in the village to provide a variety of leisure activities, as well as other organisations such as the school, church and the much under-funded air ambulance. We ran various draws, such as guess the name of the toy Easter rabbit, and quizzes, including the one where you had to make as many words as possible out of the letters contained in the words "The Village Shop" but each word had to include the letter 'g'. This proved very popular and the winner had a staggering number of words in excess of 250 – but she was an undergraduate on vacation who had scoured the internet for her impressive list. Needless to say, we did not check their accuracy, we just gave her the prize!

Our most ambitious project was one I undertook in 1998 to raise funds for the village Feast Day, equivalent to a village fete, and that was to compile a village recipe book. We invited residents to provide their favourite recipes and I, somewhat ambitiously, said I would type them up and we would copy and bind them in the shop. This turned out to be a much bigger job than I had anticipated because the response was so enthusiastic and, having asked for contributions, we could hardly leave some of them out! In the end I managed to word process them all and get them in a common format and then we ran a competition for the design of the cover. Because we could not afford to reproduce coloured designs, the winning design was drawn in black and white by Jim Reynolds, a retired engineer, who came up with a very attractive pen and ink drawing of a variety of food items. Again we could not afford to have these professionally bound so we decided on slide-on binders with a clear, cellophane front and back cover. This was an excellent idea in the planning stage but not so good, we found, in the production stage! Many an irreverent word was muttered as we struggled to feed these pages and covers into the binders only to get two thirds of the document successfully in and find the first third slipping out again! Eventually we completed sufficient to put on sale on Feast Day and they were quite a success. The binding however became problematical again when people started flicking through the books and the pages decided to disengage themselves from the spine! Nevertheless, purchasers were quite forgiving as they wanted to see their names in print as well as reading what their neighbours considered to be a good recipe! The books made a significant contribution towards Feast Day funds but, given the effort, we did rather wonder whether it would not have been easier just to write a cheque!

Help is at Hand

When we had first opened the shop we had made the decision that we would run it by ourselves. We had two main reasons for this decision. The first was that we felt that, having never run a shop before, we really had to learn the business ourselves before we involved anyone else. The second reason was financial, as we were not sure initially that we would be able to afford to employ staff and we had to let the trading position settle down before we took anyone on. Whilst we had been very encouraged by our early weeks of business we were not sure how much of that was initial curiosity and whether we could convert that into regular trade.

By November 1996 we had come to two conclusions. The business could support the employment of one member of staff and if we did not get someone to help us soon we were going to keel over! We decided that the main area in which we needed help was the shop itself, as opposed to the Post Office. I had taken on the job of Sub Postmaster and, as I had become more acquainted and comfortable with it, I had familiarised Keith in its operation. We thought this was sensible not only from the point of view of the "two heads being better than one" principle when I hit a problem but it also meant that the Post Office could remain open even if I was unwell. However, the idea of employing someone from outside to help in the Post Office had a number of drawbacks at this early stage. I would have had to formally train them from scratch, I would have had to take full financial responsibility for their actions if anything went wrong when I was not there and we would have had to pay them ourselves. There was no allowance from the Post Office for additional permanent salaries if we decided we needed to take someone on to help us. We had to meet the cost out of the salary I received from the Post Office, around £7500 per annum, and any profits we made in the shop. This was not a decision to take lightly therefore and at this early stage we decided to confine our staff support to the shop alone.

We hit gold from the very start. Our first member of staff, Catherine Mathew, had been born and brought up in the village and she was an ardent supporter of all village institutions and activities. From day one she became an invaluable member of staff who almost became a member of the family and her efforts, support and initiative played a major role in our lives as village shopkeepers. Catherine, and her husband, John, will be referred to in a number of the following chapters and she stayed with us until we sold the shop in 2003 when she left to concentrate on helping her father on the family farm.

Catherine's main role in the early days was to help us price up deliveries, stack shelves, clean shelves, check on dates of perishable stock and serve behind the counter. Over the course of the next twelve months she became so proficient at looking after all aspects of the shop, including placing orders for us, that we started to contemplate taking a holiday. From time to time we had used various youngsters in the village, who wanted Saturday jobs, to bolster the workforce, namely a brother and sister, Rebecca and Tom Chiplen, as well as Caroline Starks, a young mother looking for some occasional part-time work. We knew, therefore, that we had help which we could call upon to support Catherine if we went away and Pam and Colin were still doing the Sunday paper round so they could also be called upon to help. The dilemma was the Post Office. I had been told that the Post

Office would pay an additional sum to cover holiday relief up to a certain number of days per year but whoever we got in to run the Post Office in my absence had to be Post Office approved, in other words an existing or retired Sub Postmaster.

Our first port of call in trying to find someone to help was a charming retired Sub Postmaster, Den, from a neighbouring village, Corton Denham. Den and his wife had only recently retired and closed their shop and Post Office but we had already made contact with them and Den had offered to help any time he could. A foolish offer to make, which we took him up on and which, luckily, he was happy to agree to.

Having got all our help in place, we tentatively approached Catherine and asked her if she would be prepared to run the shop for a week in our absence. Once she heard the line up of assistance on offer and once she had the agreement of her husband, John, to help her with the early morning newspapers, she gave us the go-ahead. So, in October 1997 we left the shop with some feeling of trepidation as we set off for a week of sun and relaxation in Majorca. One thing that became apparent in the lead up to this holiday, and this is no reflection on Catherine's ability, was that there was an enormous amount of preparation which we had to do before we went away. There were a whole load of things that Keith and I did in the business which we had to either detail for Catherine to do whilst we were away, make arrangements for them not to happen during that week or try and complete before we left. For instance, we still did a lot of the ordering and therefore we had to either anticipate demand and order in before the holiday or leave detailed instructions on how and when to place the order in our absence. Nevertheless, we left feeling that we had hopefully covered every possible angle and, after all, we were only going for a week.

On our return we need not have worried! Catherine and Den had managed admirably with all their other helpers and we had had our first real break for eighteen months. Two things struck us, however, after this holiday. Firstly, not only was there an enormous amount of preparation before we went but there was an inevitable backlog of work when we got back. Again this was not Catherine's fault. Things like the accounting books had not been completed for a week and this was additional work to carry out; certain cleaning jobs which I did in the shop were outstanding simply because there had not been enough time to do them; the banking had to be done which was a regular job in Sherborne linked to collecting or delivering dry cleaning. In addition, and not unreasonably, Catherine usually booked a holiday herself to coincide with our return. Given that she normally only worked part-time and covering our holiday meant very long full-time hours, she was definitely in need of a rest by the time we came back. The downside, however, was that, having come back fully refreshed, we were launched into working longer hours than normal because we had no staff help! This whole pattern never changed over the seven years we were in the shop and there were times when the work involved either side of a break seemed to almost nullify the effect of the holiday. Almost but not entirely!

The second thing that struck us was that whilst Den had coped very well with the Post Office, that was the only role he had been employed to carry out. When Keith or I were serving in the Post Office, if custom dried up we helped in the shop, be it serving, pricing or stacking shelves. Catherine had had none of that support and it was obvious that this was not an ideal situation. Whilst we had been on holiday we had been discussing the staffing situation, particularly in respect of the Post Office, and we now felt that we had the expertise and, more importantly, the finances to employ someone part-time in the Post

Office to give us extra coverage and flexibility. The problems Catherine had experienced in our absence only further emphasised the need to sort out the Post Office staffing and in early 1998 we advertised for a Post Office Assistant.

Being a small team and having a definite ethos of wanting shopping and working in the shop to be enjoyable, we were very careful about who we took on. Having carried out interviews we settled on a bubbly lady, Gwen Hustwayte, who, with her husband, John, rented a house in the village. Gwen had some rusty Post Office experience but she was quick to learn and soon became a valuable member of the team. John and Gwen loved walking which was a good thing because their pet dog, Faroe, was an enormous black Newfoundland. He had the most gorgeous glossy black coat but he also had the habit of dribbling from his big floppy joules, which was not always too pleasant. He was about the size of a Shetland pony, very soppy but also very strong.

There was one occasion when I inadvertently nearly caused Gwen and John a serious problem. One Sunday morning, I was doing the newspaper delivery with Colin Hilton as Pam was away. It was around 8.30 a.m. in the morning and we went up to the part of the village where Gwen and John were living at the time. It was a narrow country lane which contained just two detached houses, one of which Gwen and John were renting, and ended in a cul-de-sac comprising three houses made from a barn conversion. As we went past Gwen and John's house, we were surprised to see a self-drive removal van outside. We carried on and did our deliveries at the barn conversion and took a good look at the removal van on the way back. There was no sign of anyone loading it but the tail-gate was down and there appeared to be a quantity of furniture and belongings in the van. Colin and I found it strange that there should be a van parked outside someone's house at that time on a Sunday morning and we expressed our concerns to Keith when we got back to the shop. Incidences of lorries turning up at country houses and illegally removing furniture and effects without anyone apparently reporting anything unusual were often reported in the local press and we did not want to shirk our responsibilities. We therefore telephoned the local police and expressed our concerns.

The outcome was that Gwen and John who, unbeknown to us, were moving house within the village that weekend had a visit from the local constabulary! Once they had satisfied the police that they were the rightful owners of the contents of the removal van which they had hired, they were allowed to get on with moving house! We felt rather embarrassed at the problems which we had caused but Gwen and John were very good natured about it – after, of course, they had well and truly pulled our legs!

At the time of Gwen's appointment, we formally made Catherine our Shop Manager and altered her hours. The new working pattern meant that, when we closed the shop at lunchtime on Sunday, we did not work in the shop again until first thing Tuesday morning. This was wonderful because, for the first time, it gave us nearly a whole weekend off! The only downside was when there was a Bank Holiday which meant that not only did we have to work on the Monday but we also lost our Bank Holiday whilst our staff had the day off! That aside, the arrangement worked very well and we settled down to a more civilised working pattern. It seemed to be too good to be true, and it was! In June 1998, just six months after she had started, Gwen handed in her notice as she and John had decided to move to France. To say we were disappointed would be an understatement but given Gwen's developing arthritis problem we could fully understand the draw of a warmer climate. We bade Gwen a fond farewell and to this day we still receive Christmas cards from her and John with continued offers of a bed for the night if we ever fancy a trip to France!

Gwen had been very fair to us and given us reasonable notice of her intended departure and we had advertised again for a suitable replacement. This time we attracted an applicant, Wendy Furneaux, who lived in a nearby village, Charlton Musgrove. Wendy soon picked up the idiosyncrasies of the Post Office as well as the day to day routine of the shop. She was a lovely lady but found the relentless pressure of dealing alternately with Post Office and shop tasks not really to her liking. This was a shame because she related well to the customers and we all found her very pleasant to work with.

As a result, in July 1999 – what was it about July? – Wendy announced that she would be leaving as she had found another job doing something completely different. Here we were again, placing another advert and conducting more interviews. Maybe we could pick someone this time who would stay. Two ladies from outside the village applied for the post, both of whom had previous Post Office experience and both of whom looked suitable. I arranged to interview them on the same morning as I thought comparison would be easier that way – as well as it not straining my overloaded memory too much! The first lady was a smart, attractive blond who was, at that time, working in a town Post Office so she was completely au fait with current Post Office procedures. The only disadvantage, which she very honestly told me about, was that she and her husband were in the process of selling their house and they were not quite sure where they were going to move to. It could be that they would end up further from Charlton Horethorne than they currently were in which case the travelling would become a problem.

The second lady arrived, again smartly dressed, red-haired and initially, I thought, rather severe looking. However, as we talked she started to relax and I put her earlier demeanour down to nerves. She lived in a nearby hamlet and again had Post Office experience but it was several years out of date as she had been working as a playgroup assistant whilst her own children grew up. I ended this second interview having told both applicants that I would call them that afternoon. Over lunch I told Keith how the interviews had gone and how I was really torn between a fully qualified Post Office Assistant who might not join us because of her domestic circumstances and a local lady with rusty Post Office skills but no personal complications.

"I think we should pick the lady who we know that, barring any unforeseen circumstances, will stay with us", Keith said.

"Right, it's Sue, then", I said. "At least we won't have any trouble remembering her name!"

That afternoon I made the telephone calls and Sue Bubb expressed delight that she was being offered the post. It turned out to be one of the best decisions we ever made. It is amazing how appearances can be deceptive and when, at some later date, I told Sue how she had come over at interview she admitted that she had been extremely nervous and this had made her very tense. The truth about Sue's personality was that she was fun, bubbly, full of mischief, good at her job and the customers adored her. Particularly the men. Sue would outrageously pull the legs of some of our male customers. They thought they were being very subtle when they visited the Post Office, for the most spurious reasons, when Sue was on duty. Little did they realise how predictable they were being or how much Sue was teasing them. And what she said about them when they finally left the shop would certainly have brought colour to their cheeks! Sue was not only fun to be with but she was conscientious and loyal and always very concerned about our elderly and infirm customers. She and Catherine also got on like a house on fire but there were times when even Catherine was left speechless at Sue's comments to some of our younger and more attractive male delivery men, particularly in summer when they were wearing shorts! None of this was at all offensive, just good natured bantering and made work, and even some of our more difficult customers, enjoyable!

New and Changing Suppliers

Once we had opened and settled into a reasonable pattern of trading we began to take on new suppliers and change some of our existing ones for those which we felt better suited our customers. It would be very tedious to just list those that we engaged or changed in the first two years of business. However, in most case, there were small human stories attached to these changes which made them memorable and, on occasions, amusing.

One local firm whose products we stocked from the very early days was Puddings and Pies, a reasonably descriptive company name! They sold quiches and flans, desserts and pies, cakes and pastries and up-market ready meals which came frozen. The vast majority of what they made was absolutely delicious and it was always very difficult to chose which of their large range of products to stock. One of our regular orders was for the yummy apricot slices and date slices which they made and which would be delivered in slabs. We then wrapped each slice individually in clingfilm so that they could be sold separately. Wrapping the slices was a much fought over job because inevitably, by sheer chance, odd corners of individual slices would fall off. These, of course, could not be wasted and whoever managed to bag the job of doing the wrapping would often appear afterwards, behind the counter, unaware of the tell-tale crumbs lurking around their mouth.

At the less salubrious end of the cake market was a firm, which shall remain nameless, which would deliver pre-packed cakes of the mass-produced variety, on a fortnightly basis, from a van which looked as though it had definitely seen better days. Goodies such as Swiss rolls, chocolate crackles, coconut snowballs and Battenburg cake would come off the van in cases and whilst they appealed to a minority of our customers, we had severe doubts about the quality and ingredients of cakes that appeared to have about a six-week shelf life. We also found that no sooner was a new line brought in, which our customers seemed to enjoy, than it disappeared off their stock list. The whole thing did not seem to be working very well and we told them that we no longer required them to call. They did not take this too happily and pestered us with calls and special offers for weeks until they finally got the message that we were not going to budge!

One of our customers, Mary Willingale, approached us one day and asked us if we could start to stock Miles Tea. This was not a make we had heard of but she assured us that a number of people she knew bought it from a delicatessen in Sherborne and they would definitely buy it from us if we would stock it. Nothing daunted we contacted the supplier and found that the centre of the tea and coffee industry in Somerset was none other than Bridgwater! We started to stock their tea, eventually expanding to include their coffee and, true to her word, our customer, and others, regularly bought the Miles products. We now see that Sainsbury's in Sherborne stock the full range of Miles beverages so, where The Village Shop leads Sainsbury's follows!

Early in our shop-keeping days we had gauged that there was a market for ready made sandwiches and, not wanting to get into the delicatessen business and all the regulations that involved, we engaged a company called Bunters from Yeovil to deliver daily sandwiches and rolls to us on a sale or return basis. Having this sort of product on sale or return was marvellous as consumption was always difficult to predict. Our only problem with the arrangement was when we forgot to give the delivery driver the returns which we had removed from the chill cabinet, we would then discover a packet of hairy sandwiches lurking in the fridge in the back store! He was always very good about it though and knocked the value off that day's delivery. He did however balk at taking the evidence back to the depot and always asked us to dispose of the offending item as we saw fit! The company was, when we took them on, run by a gentleman who subsequently retired and handed the business over to his step-daughter, Julie. Julie was an efficient businesswoman with a good trade in the area. However, we did have the occasional run-in with her when our sales of sandwiches did not measure up to what she thought they should be or the returns we sent back to her were higher than she wanted. In general, however, we got on very well with her and we used her business for the seven years we owned the shop. Her main delivery man was an engaging Irishman called Joe. Joe was a short, grey haired man in his late fifties with a grey beard and a twinkling Irish eye. He was also a leading member of an Irish folk band and when he was not calculating how many chicken tikka and cheese and pickle sandwiches we needed, he was recounting tales of his latest gig. On one occasion we were visiting our favourite pub, The Mitre in Sandford Orcas, and telling the landlords Alan and Cheryl about Joe. They asked whether we thought Joe's band would be interested in featuring in an Irish evening they were planning at the pub? The upshot of this was a fully orchestrated Irish evening in Sandford Orcas featuring our sandwich delivery man!

As we became more established we became the target for area reps. Some of these we greeted with enthusiasm but an awful lot were the cause of a distinct sinking feeling. They were usually middle-aged men in cheap suits, creased after spending the day driving around the county, and they carried oversized briefcases, like those used by barristers, which contained innumerable pictures and samples of their products. Getting rid of the unwanted callers was an art we had to develop over the years but it was always a trial of verbal strength.

This was never more so than on one occasion when, just before Christmas, a man turned up in an estate car, parked outside and staggered into the shop carrying boxes of Christmas confectionery. He then regaled Keith with promises of over 100% profit on everything we bought from him. Apart from the fact that we were not at all sure where this stock had come from, Keith spent a long time convincing him that we were not interested because we already had our Christmas stock. It seemed impossible to get through to him that we would only make 100% profit if we sold everything we bought from him. As this appeared far from certain, our profit margin would be considerably smaller, if anything at all! He eventually gave up and left the shop muttering to himself.

Confectionery was an area where special deals could be negotiated with the main manufacturers and we entered into such a deal with Nestle. Under this arrangement, we would qualify for two cases of free confectionery, every two months, from Nestle in return for stocking a certain number of their different lines. These lines also had to be displayed centrally on our confectionery shelves. This latter requirement was one which we did not always abide by, much to the dismay of our Nestle rep. We would organise our confectionery according to size, space, current stock levels and best-sellers, which did not always feature the required number of Nestle lines. We would always apologise profusely when the rep visited and then allow her to re-arrange our display. This had the added advantage that she would ask for a duster and we would get our shelves cleaned! Needless to say, once the rep had left the shop, the display gradually reverted, over the weeks, to its previous unstructured layout until, that is, her next visit!

Three representatives who were "cold callers" turned out to be long-term partners with us and we would almost certainly never have come across them any other way. Firstly, there were the reps from the Original Poster Company. I somewhat unkindly nicknamed them Ken and Barbie and so popular did these private nicknames become that we and our staff had to concentrate really hard not to use them in their presence. I am not sure I ever knew their real names but they were a married couple. She was blonde, in her forties, immaculately made-up and dressed with manicured nails and a softly spoken voice. He was of a similar age, wore a smart dark suit, which had not suffered the rigours of our other male reps, had immaculately cut dark hair, a dark moustache and a classy hint of aftershave. They were actually very charming but they were so courteous and indulgent in their interest in what we were doing and so politely overawed at the sales of their cards that we had achieved, they were a bit hard to take seriously. The business they ran involved providing very good quality greetings cards and stationery on a sale or return basis. They supplied two attractive stands, fully stocked them – and then went away! After about six to eight weeks they came back, calculated what we had sold, we paid them and they restocked the stands. An excellent arrangement. Their cards proved to be extremely popular and people came from far and wide to buy a selection to keep for future use. A very successful product range which also had its amusing side.

Next a very earnest young man appeared in the shop one day carrying the obligatory large briefcase. We put on our indulgent "we will give you five minutes to prove yourself" smiles and he started on his sales pitch. This time, however, we were completely hooked. The company was called Dart Valley Foods, not from Devon as the name would imply but from Winchester, and they supplied a wonderful range of jams, preserves, marmalades, pickles and chutneys as well as a chocolate spread to die for! Apart from the quality of the produce, the other appealing aspect of their range was that we could produce our own label which would mean the goods would be sold as "produced for The Village Shop, Charlton Horethorne". This really sparked our imagination and we undertook to get back to Dart Valley as soon as we had decided how we wanted to proceed. The decision was tempered by the fact that, for the one- off conversion of our artwork to pot lid covers and labels, we had to pay £250. We thought long and hard and, given that I enjoyed drawing and painting and could produce the original artwork without incurring extra cost, we decided to go ahead. It was one of the best decisions we ever took. We were so excited when our first consignment arrived with our own labels and pot lid covers and, from the beginning, the range proved to be an amazing success. Customers liked the produce anyway but the ability to buy something of quality with "The Village Shop's" name on it and take it, for instance, as a gift for a host or a relative was extremely popular. The pinnacle of this range's popularity was when a customer asked us to make up a box of Village Shop produce and send it to her family in America for Christmas. We carefully selected traditional British Christmas fare such as mincemeat, mince pies, chutneys and pickles as well as a Christmas pudding. We packed the contents with great care in bubble-wrap and then in a sturdy cardboard box. The accompanying customs declaration had to be carefully completed to avoid any confusion between the preserve, mincemeat, and minced beef, which would certainly have been destroyed on arrival! We subsequently learnt that our British Christmas food parcel had arrived safely, and on time, and had been very much appreciated. We felt very sophisticated having entered the export market!

Our third welcome cold-call visitor was a lady who brought with her a range of stationery and giftware that could be customised so that it showed illustrations of views or buildings in the village. There was nothing available at that time which visitors could buy, apart from our Dart Valley range, that related to the village of Charlton Horethorne. The lady whose business it was would take photographs around the village and then we could choose which images we would like on which products. We opted for a four-view postcard and some small porcelain bells and thimbles showing an image of the village church and the name "Charlton Horethorne". We timed the production of these latter items for the autumn, to hopefully catch the Christmas trade, although we viewed the postcards as a longer-term standard product range. The porcelain items proved to be very popular, as we had hoped, and customers really liked the idea of a small gift item from their village. The postcards were a more summer-season purchase but we sold all our original production and then found that, unfortunately, the lady we had used in the first instance was no longer in business. That meant that we had to take our own photos of the village and, using a local printer, produce our own version. This proved to be a successful alternative although it took a lot longer to organise!

We continued to expand our range of goods and suppliers over the first two years of operation. We took on an excellent cheese supplier, Hawkridge, from Devon who would provide everything from pre-packed weighed cheese to whole cheeses and who was a supplier of the much coveted Dorset Blue Vinney cheese – a creamier version of Stilton. Fudges Bakery joined our list of producers with their fabulous range of specialist sweet and savoury biscuits and their cakes. Fudges are located at Stalbridge, a mere fifteen minute drive from Charlton Horethorne, but they supply the best shops in this country including Fortnum and Mason and Harrods and also export their products all over the world. It was wonderful to have such a quality supplier on our doorstep, particularly as they were always such pleasant people to deal with. Sun Cottage were located a little further away, in Dorchester, but again they were a quality supplier with a wide range of wholegrain, organic cereals, mueslis, dried fruits, snacks and nuts. Their produce was very popular with the "organic set" as well as those hostesses who were running parties and wanted something different in the way of nibbles!

On the fringes of the normal product range carried by the shop, we needed to find a supplier of batteries and we came across a company called Mendip Batteries, from Shepton Mallet, which was owned by a very cheery man called Dave Pugh. Dave was in his fifties, tall, grey-haired with a moustache – and a real leg-puller. Keith and he had a regular banter every month when he called to restock our batteries and he often spent half an hour in the shop cracking jokes and telling stories about some of his other customers. I dread to think what he said about us!

Another slightly different product we started to stock was seeds from a producer called Fothergills. As I mentioned earlier, the village had a flourishing Gardening Club as well as a wide range of gardens from the massive ones verging on estates to the small back gardens of the pensioners' bungalows. Fothergills supplied a stand and a range of flower and vegetable seeds which they believed was suitable for a shop of our size. Most of what they supplied was very popular but their packets of wild flower seeds, presumably geared towards town dwellers trying to reproduce a slice of the countryside, were not so popular. The consensus was that most of us in the countryside tried to keep these out of our flower beds rather than paying good money to import them!

A staple of any convenience shop is the supply of milk and you would think that, living in the country, this would not be a problem. Wrong! When we first came to Charlton Horethorne, there were at least three milking herds in the village but, ten years later, there is only one left. Even when there were three herds it was impossible to buy village milk for the shop as it all had to be collected by tankers and taken to depots for pasteurisation and bottling and then it was distributed far and wide. The retail price charged for milk was always a bone of contention with the farmers, who appeared to be getting less and less for their milk whilst the retail price continued to rise. We were very aware of this, particularly as a number of our customers were farmers and their families, and we were very careful when it came to pricing our milk. Over our tenure of the shop, our dairy changed a number of times. This was not at our behest but because smaller dairies were either bought out by bigger ones or they decided to give up the milk business and passed their customers on to other dairies. We moved from Lordswood to Hambledon to Peninsula dairies but at least they were all located in the South West, the furthest, Peninsula, being located in Devon. We did also manage, during our seven years, to lower the price of our milk and then keep it at that level which earned us a lot of kudos with both our buying public and the farming community.

Arts and Crafts

When we first opened, I had the idea of providing a showcase for local artists and craftspeople to display their work and for us to sell on their behalf. To this end, we bought a glass-fronted, lockable cabinet as part of our shop fitting purchases and I publicised the idea before we opened. Unfortunately, although there proved to be a wealth of talent in the village, the idea did not take off and we ultimately took off the glass doors and just used the cabinet as an addition to our normal shelving.

Whilst this was disappointing, we did have a number of our customers who asked if we would try selling their wares. The first to make such a request was a retired Army colonel who was a semi-professional photographer. He had taken some stunning photographs around the village and had found a supplier who had transposed them onto placemats and coasters for him. He asked us if he could display them in the shop and any resultant orders would attract a commission for us. We were happy to give this a go but, although we did take some orders, possible purchasers seemed to be put off by the price. It soon became apparent that, when someone tries to enter a market like this, quantity will always drive the price down and if you do not order in quantity on the initial run, the individual prices will be too high. We did our best for our customer but it did not turn out to be a roaring success.

One existing village item that we were asked to carry was a book written by another retired Army gentleman (it must be in the genes) on the history of Charlton Horethorne. The author, the late Robert Williams, had carried out extensive research and had acquired a wide range of fascinating photographs to produce a very nicely bound book which has become the bible for anyone wanting to know anything about the history of the village. I am not sure how many were printed in the initial print run but the number was substantial and this meant that the price of £5.95 was very reasonable. We took a small commission for selling them, with the remainder of any profit being split between the church and the village school. Catherine's father, Michael Hole, was responsible for storing the boxes of unsold copies after the early flurry of interest when the book was published in 1990. We were delighted to sell the books for him as they were of interest to villagers and visitors alike and Michael was a regular visitor in the shop enquiring earnestly whether we needed any more copies? I think he was not only keen to try and recoup some of the initial printing costs but he was also desperate to reduce the stockpile and reclaim some space at home.

Other books relating to the area were produced and sold in the shop, particularly as our ownership spanned the millennium which was a catalyst for a number of local projects. Both Blackford and Sigwells, small villages within a five mile radius of Charlton Horethorne, produced books about the villages and their occupants and we were happy to be able to help them to sell them. They also proved to be a source of knowledge for us both about the villages concerned and their residents, many of whom were our customers!

In the summer after we opened, one of our customers arrived on a sunny Saturday morning and started to unload some fairly large looking objects from his boot. Keith went out to investigate and found Bill Whetstone proudly displaying a range of wooden plant troughs which he had made and which he thought we might be interested in offering for sale. Keith suggested that maybe one might be sufficient, bearing in mind that he had to hump the offending item in and out of the shop every time we opened and closed, and that it might look better planted up rather than empty. Bill readily agreed and over the following few weeks we displayed the trough and sold one or two for him. Eventually we decided that we might as well buy the trough we had had on display, we had after all grown to know it rather well over the weeks, and, if necessary, having bought it, we could leave it outside the shop and risk its theft rather than tortuously moving it twice a day! On a similar theme, another customer of ours, John Jones, turned up one day with a range of miniature wooden wheelbarrows in which to display plants. This came as quite a surprise to us as we had no idea that this was a hobby of John's and the samples he brought down were delightful. Their other advantage was that they were small and light!

One artist from outside the village who turned up out of the blue was a man called John Doulton. John lived and worked in Devon and he was a very gifted wild life artist who had produced a range of greetings cards depicting his paintings of wild birds. These cards were lovely and very popular and even though my initial idea of displaying arts and crafts had not come to fruition, we were at least giving the opportunity to this artist and others to show off their talents.

Sue and Keith in the newly-opened shop with some of their first customers

The shop fully stocked

2004 Production of Sue's Pantomime "The Adventures of Peter Rabbit"

Keith as "Hamish MacGregor" and Charlotte Burrough as "Marmaduke"

Pat Bunter as "Mrs Rabbit" and Denise Cooper as "Mr Rabbit"

Sue and Keith's Charlton Horethorne Garden Show exhibits and their totally unexpected certificate of success !

Banksian  Medal

PRESENTED BY

The Royal Horticultural Society

AND AWARDED BY
CHARLTON HORETHORNE & DISTRICT GARDENING CLUB

TO

KEITH GUDGEON
SUE BROWNING

for the largest total amount of prize money/points in the whole of the horticultural classes.

(Winners in previous two years excluded.)

SUMMER SHOW 1997

Fun With The Customers

Life in the shop had its ups and downs but the ups were predominant and often revolved around the people with whom we dealt, customers, staff and suppliers. Some of the incidents that occurred were ones where we laughed with the individuals concerned but some were things that happened that caused us great amusement which was not necessarily shared with the person causing it!

The knowledge of some of our customers, particularly it has to be said retired professional men, when it comes to food shopping left something to be desired. We had one customer for whom greengrocery was a completely alien world. He once came to the counter with a large, round, dark green cabbage and asked "Is there a cauliflower in there?"

Not an easy question to answer with a straight face. However, he excelled himself when, on another occasion he came forward brandishing a leek and a stick of celery and asked "Which one of these is celery?"

When Sue and Catherine worked in the shop there was never any doubt that there would be a lot of laughter but on one occasion we were all reduced to tears. One of our lady customers, the-ex wife of a vicar, lived on her own with two dogs and a cat plus assorted fowl in the garden. She was a lady in her 60's who rode a bicycle with the two dogs in tow and she was one of those people who, when you were talking to her, sometimes did not quite grasp the meaning of what you were saying. Equally, she would sometimes arrive in the shop and carry on about a subject which you could only assume she had previously been discussing with the dogs because she started off mid-story meaning that, most of the time, we did not have a clue what she was talking about! On this particular morning, I was stacking shelves, Keith was in the back store and Sue and Catherine were behind the counter when she came over to be served. This lady usually went to Scotland for a month in summer to go bird-watching and, for something to say, Sue asked her if she was going to Scotland in the near future.

"No," she replied. "I can't this year because my pussy is getting too old!"

I looked at Sue and she looked at me and we started to giggle and we were soon so convulsed we had to go out to the back store leaving Catherine to complete the transaction with a straight face. What made it so difficult was that the lady concerned had no idea what she had said. Once she had left the shop, Catherine came out to the back and said "You rotten pair leaving me there on my own."

We could not say anything, we had tears pouring down our faces and Keith was standing beside us trying to get some sense out of us as he did not have a clue what was going on!

In a similar vein, not long after we had opened, a farming landowner who lived opposite us came in one afternoon and started hunting around on the shelves for something. Not immediately finding what he was looking for he came to the counter and asked if we stocked Vaseline. I pointed him to the shelf just behind him and he said "Oh, excellent. I need it for the ram!" The mind boggled but I did not have the nerve to enquire further so I just took his money and let my imagination run wild for the rest of the afternoon.

Security in the shop became an issue from time to time but we were reasonably happy that we had a good security system to cover us for most eventualities. The efficiency of the system was demonstrated to us one morning in a rather unfortunate manner. We had two sets of personal attack alarms behind the counter which we were assured by the installers would link straight through to the police station for an immediate response. We were also assured that they would be difficult to set off accidentally. Not so on this occasion! For reasons that I am not sure we ever found out, the personal attack alarm in the Post Office was triggered accidentally one morning. All hell broke out with the external alarm making the most horrendous noise. Whilst we were in the midst of telephoning the alarm company control centre to tell them that it was a false alarm, we heard a screeching of tyres and brakes and looked out of the shop window to see two police patrol cars. They had drawn to a halt at angles across the back and front of a workman's van which was parked outside the shop and policemen were piling out dressed in bullet-proof vests. The poor individual, who was sat in the van innocently sticking onto letters the second class stamps which he had just bought in the Post Office, looked shell-shocked and ashen! After a few minutes consultation with the police, we convinced them that we were not under siege and that the workman should be allowed to go about his lawful business.

The road outside the shop also provided a number of areas of amusement, not least the livestock. The manor farm opposite the shop was home to a large number of chickens and ducks who, from time to time, used to wander about the lanes and particularly across the main road through the village. On more than one occasion we had strangers to the area coming into the shop in a very concerned state saying that there were ducks or chickens on the road and what were we going to do about it? Our usual response was "Nothing. They're our traffic calming measure!" And this was true. Traffic never slowed down for elderly people or children walking through the village but even smart sports cars came to a grinding halt to allow a hen and her chicks across the road! The owner of these fowl did not mind them wandering around the lanes but she did not like it when, for instance, the pub next door to us started putting out scraps for them. Not only was it not necessarily the best food for them but it encouraged them to cross the road more than they might otherwise have done and although they usually achieved this successfully they were not always lucky. For this reason, when, one afternoon, the lady concerned came over to shop with us and, much to her consternation, found one of her best hens on our side of the road, she dealt with the matter in the obvious way. Rather than walk all the way back to the farmyard, she tucked the hen under her arm – it was very tame – and completed her shopping with the hen clucking away contentedly. It was rather difficult to carry out a normal conversation over the counter, and price up her purchases, with a hen following your every move. However, we only had a 'No Dogs' sign up so we could hardly bar the chicken!

Anyone who has seen the situation comedy series on television, "Keeping Up Appearances", will realise that some people can be a little over-powering. We had customers like this whose appearance in the shop always caused a reaction. Some could not resist joining in other people's conversations or loudly discussing, about three inches from the listener's face, some snippet of village gossip that they had overheard somewhere. The layout of the shop was such that we had a double-sided shelving unit running three quarters of the length of the shop, parallel with the counter, so that customers could browse around both sides. We actually witnessed customers coming in, not noticing a particular shopper was at the counter, and then, when they saw who was there, ducking down behind the shelving unit and mouthing to us "Has she gone yet?" We also saw cars draw up outside the shop, then the occupants would recognise a certain vehicle parked outside and they would pull away again to return later when the coast was clear!

Parking outside the shop could sometimes be difficult when we were busy and around 11.00 a.m. the Postman would arrive in his van to empty the box and take whatever we had for him to collect in the Post Office. On one occasion, Dave Sneade, the village Postman of over 20 years standing, was leaning on the counter whilst we put together his collection. The door opened and a lady from the village, June Gear, came in with her grandson, George, who was then about 3 years old and about a metre tall. George knew Dave but on this particular morning he was none too pleased with the Postman. He went straight over to where Dave was standing, looked up at his face and said in a loud and rather annoyed voice "You are parked in my granny's space!"

We all tried to hide our amusement as George viewed this as a serious issue and not one to be laughed at. Dave apologised profusely and went outside to move his offending vehicle.

Children were often a source of amusement, not least three young girls who came into the shop with their grandmother during one school summer holiday. Having been left at the counter to choose their sweets they were waiting for granny to finish her other shopping. Aged between about 4 and 8 they were getting bored at the counter so I looked at the little one and, for something to say, commented "That's a very pretty dress you are wearing."

Before she had time to respond, her eldest sister retorted "Yes, but we've all had it!"

I am not sure whether her mother or granny would have wanted that piece of information broadcast far and wide!

Keith had made it his personal mission to try and improve the local children's mental arithmetic! It was very obvious that some of them handed over their money without a clue about how much change they should get and Keith, being very good at those sorts of calculations, used to tease them into working out the right answer. On a couple of occasions, however, this backfired on him. One afternoon, a local grandfather, Arthur While, brought his grandson aged about 7 into the shop and treated him to penny sweets. These were very popular with the children but could sometimes be a pain to sell when they wanted two or three of each variety! Nevertheless, on this afternoon the choice had been made, money had been handed over and Keith looked at the lad and said "Well, how much change do you want?"

Expecting a furrowed brow and a mathematical answer Keith was dumbfounded by the response, "All of it!"

The other occasion when Keith was caught out was again when serving penny sweets. It was our habit, with regular young customers, to be not too accurate about the number of sweets we counted out – if they had asked for 12 often 15 or so were dropped into the bag. One grandmother came in to the shop one day with a story that she thought would amuse us. Her granddaughter was a regular purchaser of penny sweets and hence was a regular beneficiary of our generosity. However, what we did not know was that she went home and counted her sweets before she ate them, presumably to make sure she had received her money's worth! Having discovered the excess in the bag, she had commented to her granny that it was very sad because the man in the shop could not count! So much for generosity and mental arithmetic.

At the other end of the age spectrum, our older customers often gave us cause for amusement. Not long after we moved into the cottage and we were living out of virtually one room, we began to notice an older man paying regular visits to the skip which, at that time, was a permanent feature outside the house. The gentleman in question was short, always wore a peaked cap and pushed an empty pram with a small Jack Russell in tow on a piece of string. The builders had commented that he was a frequent visitor to the skip but that they had not deterred him as he only seemed to be taking pieces of wood out and, in any case, he was making more space for them! Once we had opened, our scavenger became a regular customer and we always knew when he was in the shop because he sang to himself as he went around. Keith dreaded serving him because his West Country accent was so strong that Keith frequently had to call on Catherine or me to interpret. Sadly, during the time we owned the shop, this gentleman died and when his bungalow was cleared his relatives found his back garden stacked high with pieces of wood for his fire. He obviously was concerned that, one day, he might be left with no means of keeping himself warm.

Another senior citizen became a regular customer of ours not long after we opened. He was a tall, upright, grey-haired man with a soft Somerset accent and gentle country ways. When he started coming to us he was already in his nineties and although his relatives did a lot of his shopping for him outside the village, he had three regular purchases – his newspaper, sherry and chocolates. Whenever he came in he always bought two or three packets of chocolates or sweets which he said he kept in the house for his grandchildren when they visited although we often thought that maybe he had a bit of a sweet tooth as well. His bottles of sherry sometimes caused us a problem. Under the terms of our off-licence we were not supposed to sell alcohol before a certain time in the morning and our elderly customer was always an early riser who came down to the shop between 7.30 a.m. and 8.00 a.m. Officially, we should not have sold him his sherry when he came in but we worked on the principle that we could hardly ask a ninety year old to pay two trips to the shop just to meet the terms of some bureaucracy. We really did not think, at his age, he was going to start a trend of early morning drinking.

One elderly lady in the village who, during our time in the shop, was virtually housebound, used to send her shopping list down via another villager and we would make up her order. Apparently this lady had, in her time, been, as they say, quite a character and had something of a reputation for liking a tipple. A regular staple of her weekly order was a bottle of our cheapest brandy. On one occasion, when we were nearing Christmas, the order went up to two bottles on the basis that she was making a lot of Christmas cakes! The comment from the villager who delivered her shopping to her was that she must be making one for each household in the village! Sadly, when she later died and her house was being cleared, numerous bottles of unopened brandy were found stashed away in cupboards.

The population of the village was, and still is, made up of people from all walks of life and with a wide range of interests. A retired lady who lived further down the road from the shop was an enthusiastic shopper in our early days and she had a wicked sense of humour. She had been a teacher who, for some time, had been a governor at the village school and she was very well read in classical literature. Her humour, however, stemmed from the fact that she was getting older and she frequently came in with sheets of jokes about old people which she offered to us to photocopy and which were, invariably, hilarious. Unfortunately her health deteriorated, she had to give up driving and her general mobility became quite limited which meant that we saw her far less often in the shop. I was therefore horrified when, one summer afternoon, I glanced out of the shop window and I saw this lady slowly making her way up the pavement on the opposite side of the road wearing fluffy pink slippers and walking with a Zimmer frame. I was obviously concerned that she might trip and fall but my horror turned to disbelief when she took a sharp right turn, stepped off the curb and started, at a snail's pace, across the road. The main road which runs through the village is a minor road but it is quite heavily used as a link between the A303 and the A30 and the 30 mile an hour speed limit is seldom respected. Luckily I had no customers in the shop at the time so I just ran out and stood in the middle of the road with my hands up and managed to stop the cars which appeared. By the time I had safely negotiated the lady across the road there were queues of three or four cars in both directions and the driver of one of the cars at the head of the queue wound down his window and jovially said to our elderly resident "You must stop running around the roads like this, love!"

When I had safely steered the lady into the shop and found her a seat, because by this time she was exhausted, I looked into the back garden where Keith had been mowing the lawn and beckoned to him to come. I told him what had happened and he stopped his gardening and got our car out and, once we had found the few things she wanted, he drove her home. None of us could cope with a return episode of jay walking!

One lady we grew very fond of whilst we were in the shop was a cross between Margaret Rutherford and Barbara Woodhouse. When we were first introduced to her we called her by her surname, as we did all our customers when we first met them until we were invited to call them by their Christian names. We later learnt that our customer had appreciated this gesture in her early dealings with us and she soon asked us to call her by her first name. She was the widow of an Army major with whom she had set up a kennel of Basset hounds which were used for hunting hares. She was highly regarded in this canine field and the hounds which she bred were sold all over the world. She drove a rather beaten up green Land Rover, with a cigarette hanging out of her mouth and if her hounds, or for that matter any of her kennel staff, did something out of order she could bellow like a regimental sergeant major! Despite all this she was a likeable person with a sharp wit and she became a very good customer of the shop. Knowing that I did all the word processing associated with our Newsletters and other shop communications, she asked me to do various pieces of typing for her associated with the hunt. I had no problem in doing this for her as she was always so generous with her custom.

The first year we were in the shop we were invited to her puppy show. We really had no idea what this entailed but we gladly accepted. On the back of this invitation was a very good order, including copious amounts of alcohol, which Keith delivered on the morning of the show. He came back with tales of a large marquee, caterers, marked out rings, chairs for spectators and all the trappings of quite a major event. We had had a panic telephone call from our customer a couple of days before the show worrying how she was going to keep drinks cool in what was turning out to be a scorching weekend. We offered to get hold of as much ice as possible and bring it up on the morning and she gratefully accepted. Keith went off to our wholesaler in Yeovil and bought as much ice as we thought we could get in our freezers which we then delivered to the site on the Saturday morning.

This lady's other problem when she held her shows was what she should wear. Her usual dress was a pair of well-worn, green corduroy trousers, a shirt or sweater and a scruffy waxed jacket. On this occasion she conceded that she should wear a dress and she always came in muttering darkly "Do you have any tights in my size? I suppose I had better wear them but I hate the bloody things!"

We were amazed, when we turned up to watch the show in the afternoon, that a number of the ladies were immaculately turned out in floral dresses and large straw hats, all the gentlemen wore ties and the stewards at the show were dressed in white, long-sleeved coats and black bowler hats. The atmosphere harked back to a pre-War era of country events which, sadly, now seem to be no more.

One way of identifying people in a village is by their dogs! Often residents met whilst out walking their pets and they would come into the shop and ask us the name of the person with such and such a breed of dog. The way some people looked upon their dogs was also an eye-opener. We had never heard of dogs having "Godparents" or sending birthday cards before we owned the shop! One customer used our fax service to send messages to a friend overseas who was the "Godparent" of her dogs. Even more worryingly, we received a reply from the dogs wishing their counterparts in Charlton Horethorne a happy birthday!

One customer had a more normal, although just as close, relationship with his dog. The customer was a landscape gardener who took his dog, a Border collie, everywhere with him in his van. During the summer, when master and dog had had a particularly long and hot day, they would call at the shop and two ice creams would be bought. Something on a stick for the owner and a tub for the dog. Then the two of them would sit outside, on the shop forecourt, and eat their ice creams.

Dogs, as everyone knows, are man's best friend but they do also tend to shed their hair over everything. One afternoon, a gentleman from a neighbouring village brought his suit in to be cleaned, saying that he thought it should be done because he was going up to London for a meeting at the end of the week. Customers used to bring their dry cleaning in over their arms, in carrier bags or even neatly on hangers but, once they had left the shop, it was all stuffed into a black bin liner for transporting to the dry cleaners in Sherborne. This occasion was no exception and the suit was bundled away with the other items already in the bag. Imagine my horror, therefore, when later that afternoon the customer rang and said his meeting had been brought forward and, whilst he realised that there would not have been time to have it cleaned, he would call at the shop in the morning to collect his suit! That evening, I spent a good half an hour pressing a none-too-pleasant suit covered in dog hairs so that the customer could have it back in the morning in at least no worse a state than he had left it! When he came in to collect the suit the following day and said something along the lines that maybe it did not look too bad after all, I just about managed to keep a straight face.

Keeping a straight face was not always possible. One of the main practical jokers in the village was Colin, who with his sister, Pam, had helped us in the early days. On a sunny afternoon during one summer, Colin called in to make a purchase and his hands were covered in scratches. When I asked him what he had been doing he said he had been pruning blackberry bushes and I stupidly made the throw-away comment that it looked as though they had been fighting back. I did not think any more about it until, about an hour later, when the shop was full of customers, in walked, or rather, hobbled Colin. His head was bandaged, his arm was in a sling and he was walking with a crutch. When I asked him what on earth had happened to him he said "It was those blackberries. When I got home they ambushed me!"

That taught me to be very careful how I phrased my words with Colin – and it also taught me how to serve customers who were strangers to the village and who thought they had just encountered a lunatic who had escaped from a local asylum!

Working in the shop only reinforced the Yorkshire saying that "there's nowt so queer as folk" and their reactions to events could be neither predicted nor on some occasions believed. In 2000, we commissioned marketing students from Yeovil College to carry out a market survey on the shop, its business, its customers and whether there were any obvious changes or improvements we could make. This exercise involved comparison with two other village shops in the area as well as personal interviews with a number of the residents in the relevant villages. One of the key findings was that the value of properties in a village with a successful shop was enhanced by 5% to 10% and Keith and I laughingly commented to ourselves that maybe we should ask for a profit share from our property-owning customers! One morning shortly after the findings of this research had been made known to the local residents, I came in to the shop to find Keith and a lawyer friend of ours who lived in the village, Tom George, doubled up in laughter with tears pouring down their faces. Apparently another gentleman, who was a local resident, had been in for his paper and the survey had become a topic of conversation between the three of them. This third person had announced that he was most unhappy about the results of the research particularly in respect of the perceived effect on the value of properties. When questioned as to his concerns, he had pronounced that this was bound to result in an increase in Council Tax! Keith and Tom were initially rendered speechless and then dissolved, when they were alone, into helpless laughter. As I said earlier, people's reactions can never be second-guessed!

Sometimes, our reactions to sales had to be kept to ourselves and discussed later in the evening over a drink. Sales to the pub, which was next door to us, fell into this category. When we first arrived in the village, the King's Arms served food, with a snack and main menus. Neither of these menus was extensive or sophisticated and the food could best be described as basic "pub grub". The food trade in the pub was not exactly brisk and, therefore, the landlord did not keep a large stock of ingredients, particularly perishable ones. This proved to be of benefit to us in the shop. When strangers pulled up, parked in the car park opposite and strolled into the pub at lunchtime, we waited for the landlord to arrive. Almost without fail, he would rush in, having left the pub by the back door, and breathlessly ask if we had the constituents for, say, a pate ploughman's lunch? We would oblige and he would return the way he had come so that he could prepare and present to his unaware customers the lunch they had ordered! In later years, under a different and increasingly unsuccessful landlord, the stock of food ingredients reduced even further. This was epitomised by some of his regular lunchtime customers, the lads from the local racing stables, being sent in with cash from the pub till to buy bags of frozen chips. These were then taken back next door to be cooked for their meal! Sadly, this deterioration in the standard of the pub continued until it finally closed in 2006 but, at the time of writing, a private purchaser has now bought it and it will hopefully soon be restored to its former glory.

Local Suppliers

We had always intended to source a large proportion of our food products from local suppliers but this did not always prove to be easy, as was shown earlier by our struggle to purchase local milk. Nevertheless, we did stock goods from a number of very local suppliers and, more often than not, they approached us rather than the other way around.

One of our customers was a farmer's wife who had a small, serve-yourself outlet for, amongst other things, flowers and plants which she grew as a sideline. During our second spring in the shop she asked us if we would like to try selling some of her bedding plants outside the shop on a shared profit basis. We were pleased to agree because not only did she produce good quality, well labelled plants but they added a definite splash of colour to the shop front. These proved to be very successful and there were times when we were literally selling the plants straight out of the cardboard boxes in which she had delivered them before we had time to display them. As we progressed through the summer and into the autumn, our supplier replaced the bedding plants with cut flowers, particularly chrysanthemums, which again proved a good seller. We ended the year with traditional pot plants such as cyclamen and, at times, she had difficulty keeping up with our requests for stock. Sadly, when the lady's husband died suddenly, she found keeping going with her plants too much and a happy business relationship ceased although she still continued to be a regular customer.

A product that we were never short of was main-crop potatoes. Our farming next-door neighbour, who had been a dairy farmer when we bought the shop, had sold the herd two or three years after we arrived. As an aside, whilst the sale of the herd was in one sense the sad end of an era for our neighbour, I do not think he regretted losing the chore of twice-daily milking and we were certainly pleased to see the back of the summer swarms of flies which were attracted to the milking parlour. The herd was actually sold in the yard which ran parallel to our garden and, on the morning of the sale, dozens of rugged, rosy-faced, flat-capped farmers arrived in a fleet of Land Rovers in the hope of making a good purchase. We could not actually see the auctioneer from the cottage but he could be easily heard as he rattled through the bidding. I must say this was the first auction where I have overheard an auctioneer saying "Now come on gentlemen, you'll never see a better set of tits than this. What am I bid?!"

Once the herd was sold, our neighbour invested in steers to be reared for beef. This had the heart-rending and somewhat annoying side-effect of calves, which he had bought in to rear and who had just been removed from their mothers, mooing all night for the first couple of nights that they were separated. An autumn ritual involved these cattle being brought in from the fields and kept in the farmyard over winter to let the ground recover. One of our annual joys was watching them being let out to graze again in the spring. I would never have believed that hefty steers could jump and cavort like little lambs if I had not seen it with my own eyes! However, back to potatoes. Apart from the beef cattle, our neighbour sowed quite a considerable acreage of potatoes each year which he normally sold by the sack load from one of his barns. These proved to be a very popular local product which we bought throughout the winter from him to the benefit of both him and us.

We were very conscious, when we first opened the shop, that we did not want to upset or offend any of our existing or potential customers. Therefore, when one of our elderly gentlemen customers asked if we would like to sell some old English varieties of apples we accepted his offer. This gentleman was an expert on rare and unusual varieties of apples and had a large orchard containing some interesting examples. Having agreed to sell some of them for him, he brought along a wide selection of different apples, suitably labelled for sale. Unfortunately, although I am sure they were all delicious in their own unique ways, by definition they were of uneven shape, quality and size and not altogether attractive to look at. Customers these days have a supermarket perception of what apples should look like and they are not very adventurous when it comes to trying something unusual, however good and interesting its pedigree. We therefore delicately extricated ourselves from buying any more of the gentleman's extensive stock whilst continuing to show as much interest as possible in his quest to preserve these ancient varieties.

A rather more bizarre offering was made one morning by a gentleman on horseback. A large, rather shaggy-looking horse, whose rider must have been in his seventies, was brought to a halt outside the shop. The rider, who wore nothing on his head, was dressed in 1940's style tweeds and he called out to us in a military voice "Would you like some courgettes? I've got far too many and I could bring some down to you."

Once again we were cautious in rejecting such an offer, for all we knew the gentleman could be a local man of influence who, if we upset him, might cause us to quickly earn a bad name. So we thanked him profusely and said we would be grateful to take some of his excess. The box of vegetables that arrived was not what you would call top rate! The first problem was that the courgettes were all bright, egg-yolk yellow! We had been accustomed to the traditional green variety and were rather taken aback by this version. We also knew that our customers were not very gastronomically brave in general and just selling courgettes was a small milestone, let alone yellow ones! The other problem was that they ranged in size from a foetal gherkin to a sizeable marrow with only a small proportion being of standard courgette size. I am afraid most of them ended up on the compost heap. We later learnt that the gentleman in question ran what, in the late 1990's, was a rather avant garde, organic food, alternative therapies, meditation etc. establishment in a neighbouring hamlet and, as such, was unlikely to ever be a significant customer in a traditional village convenience store. We therefore had no problem in turning down his other kind offers of unwanted vegetables!

One offer we never turned down, however, was that of home-grown asparagus. A customer of ours had a very large asparagus bed and, as is the way with asparagus, it has a fairly short season and it all tends to be ready for cutting within a short space of time. We ended up doing a good old fashioned form of bartering with this customer. Keith and I are both keen gardeners and one of Keith's passions is growing his own tomatoes. When we had the shop, he used to sow extra seeds and sell the plants we did not need as a sideline. However, in this case, tomato plants were readily bartered for asparagus and I am afraid most of the asparagus we received was either eaten straight away by us or frozen for later use. Our shop customers rarely had the chance of sharing this delicacy! To this day, our bartering arrangement with our asparagus grower is still going strong with tomato plants still being swapped for bundles of delicious fresh green and white shoots.

Local produce also emanated from my family. My parents had a large garden attached to their house in Sherborne and in the garden was an old Victoria plum tree. Roughly every other year this tree yielded what can only be described as a deluge of plums which, hard as they tried, my parents really could not cope with. Even after they had been eaten fresh, frozen, made into jam and given to every conceivable neighbour they still had tens of pounds of plums left over. One year the glut was such that my father brought over at least two large boxes full which we sold in the shop. Local Victoria plums proved to be very popular and we sold a significant quantity although the disadvantage, as they began to over-ripen, was the enthusiastic wasps we seemed to attract from far and wide. At one stage we were inundated with wasps and coincidentally, at the same time, a neighbouring cottage had to call in the pest control officer to rid them of a large wasps nest. We were never sure whether the nest came before the plums or vice versa.

A good customer of ours – the one with the ice-cream eating dog – ran a landscaping business and also supplied us with plants. This was a rather more hit and miss affair. One source for his plants was the gardens he was working on. He was often asked to completely re-layout a client's garden and this would mean removing perfectly good plants and shrubs. Like most gardeners, he could not bear to see good plants go to waste and he would pot them up and bring them down to us to sell. Alternatively, he would decide that a garden that he was working on required extra plants and he would grow on a large number, the surplus of which he would again bring down to us. There was only one problem with this arrangement. Our customer was an excellent hard landscaper of gardens but, by his own admission, at that time, he was not a plant man. More often than not he would bring his plants down to us and he had not the faintest idea what they were! We would then scour our gardening books trying to at least identify the variety if not the particular colour of the blooms! This was not always successful and sometimes he and we had to admit defeat and he would take his plants home to dispose of as he saw fit.

One highly successful source of local supply came about purely by chance. A customer whose husband was a very keen fisherman was standing at the counter one day bemoaning the fact that she now had two freezers full of salmon trout. Her throw-away comment of "You don't know of anyone who wants some trout, do you?" resulted in a flourishing trade for both of us. Her husband regularly fished at a trout farm in Devon, which was fed by streams running off Dartmoor and as a consequence the fish were of a very high standard. We placed a sign in the window offering West Country trout for sale and they became a very popular product. It was what the Americans call a "win, win" situation. Our customers were delighted, we and our fisherman made a modest profit and his wife started to see the bottom of her freezer again!

Home Life

In amongst all the ups and downs of running a village shop, our personal life also had its moments, mostly good but occasionally not so good. Keith had originally left his native West Yorkshire in 1986 for business life in London but he never lost his Yorkshire accent or his love for Bradford City Football Club – somewhat misplaced, some might say! His son, Richard, carried on the family tradition with even more fervour. At a distance, they shared the ups (few) and downs (many) of the ardent football supporter, culminating in the Club's two years in the Premiership. Joint visits to watch their beloved team were rare but treasured by both of them.

Another treasured opportunity was the chance to celebrate my son Richard's 18th birthday in January 1997 in our newly restored cottage (Richard is a popular name in this family!). As he had been involved from the start of the project, including taking a depressing video of the shop and cottage before refurbishment, it was good to be able to hold the celebration in our new home.

Richard, my stepson, and his wife were living in Yorkshire for most of the time that we had the shop, so getting to see them was always quite difficult. However, in 2000, they presented us with a beautiful grandson, William, the first grandchild for either of us. To say that we were delighted was an understatement and we could not wait to see him. Although it was a long journey, the family did manage to come down on several occasions and, I have to say that, owning a fully-stocked shop from which you can pick anything you like was brilliant when you had anyone staying. William, as he got older, liked the idea of grandparents who owned a shop that stocked sweets, food, drinks and comics! He also liked to see the animals when he came down to the country and he loved seeing the dogs tied up outside the shop. On one occasion, a customer, Adela Dyson, had tied up her white West Highland Terrier and we momentarily lost William. He was then spotted, sitting outside on the forecourt next to Gertie, the Terrier, with his arm over her back, saying "Hello, Goggie!"

Gertie was very placid and quite happily took this attention. The two of them sat there, taking in the scenery, looking for all the world like two little old men on a park bench! By the time we eventually sold the shop, William was able to speak to us on the telephone, although we did need some translation from his father. Within a few weeks of leaving the business, a lovely grand-daughter, Gemma, was a happy addition to the family. We now have regular telephone conversations with both of them and, despite their now living in Teesside, we see Richard, his wife, Michelle, his step-daughter, Alex, and the two little ones as often as we can. During our ownership of the shop, Richard progressed in his career, training as a Management Accountant with CEGB (National Grid), obtaining his professional management accountancy qualifications and then taking on a financial role with Magnet Kitchens. He is now Finance Director with D1 Oils, one of the companies leading the way in bio-fuels.

My step-daughter, Allison, and her husband, Liam, were married in 2000 and whilst Keith went to Guildford to give his daughter away, unfortunately I was not able to leave the shop. Keith left Charlton Horethorne early on the morning of the wedding and Catherine and I set about getting the business up and running. During the course of the morning, a very large box from Next was delivered, addressed to me, which I took to the back of the shop. When I opened it I must admit I shed a tear because it was the most wonderful bouquet of flowers from Allison and Liam saying how sorry they were I could not be with them. It really was a sweet thought.

Allison and Liam live in Guildford which meant that they were the closest to hand. With our passion for gardening, Allison was always keen to take advantage of our offers to be the "Ground Force" team and assist in the development of her's and Liam's various gardens. One of Keith's specialities, inherited from his own father, was the making of summer hanging-baskets which Allison was happy to accept and display, keeping her definitely one-up on her neighbours!

Allison had always had a love of children and therefore it was no surprise when she chose this as the basis of her career. Initially she worked as a Nursery Assistant at a local Primary School and then became a full-time Nanny to two boys in a neighbouring Surrey village. Having studied for, and achieved, an HND in Childcare, she was appointed Head Teacher of the Junior Department of a large, private Primary School in Westminster. This boasted, amongst others, the children of Messrs. Abramovich and Mourinho of Chelsea Football Club fame, so fund-raising functions at the school were always very well supported! Both Allison and Liam lead very busy lives with Liam being the National Sales Manager of Standard Life Healthcare. They still find time, however, to indulge their passion for football although they support Tottenham Hotspur, which ensures plenty of inter-family rivalry.

In 1997, my son, Richard, and I had the enormous thrill of going to St. James' Palace where he received his Gold Duke of Edinburgh Award, which he had completed before leaving school. He then set off for Cardiff University to start reading Engineering but, by December of that year, he had decided that Engineering was not for him and he transferred to Exploration Geology. However, he could not start that course until September of the following year so he returned home and got himself a job as a labourer/general factotum for a building company. The downside to this job was that he could not bear to throw things away that "might be useful" and the off-cuts of wood and endless tins of half-full paint began to mount up. When he returned to university, we began to surreptitiously dispose of our stock of "useful" building materials!

University, thankfully, proved to be much more successful the second time around, not least because Richard met his future wife, Debbie, there and they were married in October 2003, just three months after we had sold the shop. They subsequently presented us with a wonderful grandson, Oliver, in February 2007. Richard works for BP in London in methanol trading and they live near Caterham in Surrey. This is relatively close to us, compared to my stepson and his family, but, like all our children, it is further away than we would like!

Despite our geographical spread, there was one famous occasion when, for Keith's birthday, I managed to get both my step-children and their partners down to Charlton Horethorne, at the same time, as a surprise. Keith was a keen cricketer and I had managed to persuade him to play in a match on this particular weekend and I had instructed the family that they had to arrive whilst he was out. I was then concerned, all afternoon, that either the match would over-run or that he would call to say he was staying on to have a drink with the other players. Luckily neither of these things happened and he arrived home to find a house full of family and a birthday dinner in the oven!

As I mentioned earlier, my parents lived in nearby Sherborne but Keith's parents lived in a hamlet on the outskirts of Bradford in Yorkshire. We tried to get up to see them whenever we could but the commitment of the shop meant that getting away was not always easy. When we did visit, we helped Keith's father with odd jobs that he was no longer able to do in his greenhouses. In his day, he had been a keen and successful market gardener and, even when age prohibited him from the more active work, he still liked to do some pottering in the greenhouse nearest the house. Sadly, Keith's father died just over a year after we started running the shop and he was never able to see what we had achieved. However, Keith's mother was, until recently, a regular visitor despite the distance involved and she seemed to enjoy her trips to the West Country.

In 1998 my parents celebrated their Golden Wedding and had a big lunch party for all their friends and neighbours in a marquee in their garden on a beautiful sunny summer Sunday. As a family treat, and combined with a holiday for them, they invited us, my son, Richard, and a university friend of his to join them for a weekend at a hotel in Jersey. It was a very successful weekend despite the fact that Richard had just been diagnosed with glandular fever. This illness did not, however, stop him and his friend, Mike, enjoying the use of a hire car although I do not think it was quite in the plan to have him driving it at high speed on St. Brelade's beach, after dark, doing wheel spins! His grandfather was not too impressed when, on the following morning, Richard and Mike had to wash the car to remove all the sand before it could be returned to the rental company!

My father had always been very supportive of our enterprise and, being a retired businessman, could ask some searching questions about our business decisions. It was therefore very sad when he contracted a serious illness in 2001 and died in 2003, just two months before we sold the business and moved house. The help and support of our staff during that difficult time is something which we will always appreciate.

Our main happy family event was in 1999 when Keith and I were married. Our marital status, prior to this, was only raised on one occasion and this was in a manner which caused us much amusement. In our first autumn in the village we had gone into the pub next door to take part in a pub quiz and we were just buying our first drink when we were approached by a lady who was one of our customers. Obviously our relationship had been causing her much curiosity and, with her courage enhanced with alcohol, she came right out with the question "Are you brother and sister?"

We did our best not to laugh outright and confirmed that we were partners, in all senses of the word, and she drifted away having had her curiosity satisfied.

When we decided, towards the end of 1998, that we had both the time to organise and the money to finance a wedding, we had to decide what we were going to do. Although our local vicar would have been amenable to our being married in the village church we felt that, as I was widowed and Keith was divorced, this would not sit comfortably for us. However, as we are both committed Christians, we definitely wanted a religious input into our marriage. We therefore settled on a civil wedding followed by a church blessing and we set about trying to organise this. Firstly, we wanted to find a venue at which we could hold both the civil ceremony and the reception. The local registry office, whilst a very pleasant room, was in a building housing social services, tax and other government offices and did not have an exactly romantic atmosphere. We therefore obtained a list of all the venues in the area which were licensed to perform marriage ceremonies and, on our days off, we started a grand tour of the area. By the time we had seen a converted water mill which also had a tea room and visiting coach parties, a manor house with a baronial hall housing a variety of stuffed animals and vicious instruments of torture, a slightly run-down hotel with faded curtains and a stale smell of food and drink and a massive country house run by the local authority which was fully booked for the next two years, we were beginning to lose heart. The last place we visited was Charlton House in Shepton Mallet, a country house hotel run by the owners of the Mulberry company and we struck gold. The minute we crossed the bridge over the river running through the grounds, walked into the hall with the sweeping staircase and sank into the big, squishy sofas in the elegant lounge, we knew we had found the venue for our wedding. After discussing every little detail with the helpful staff we settled on Sunday 9th May for the ceremony.

As I mentioned earlier, we also wanted to have a church blessing of our marriage and we very much wanted this element of our wedding to involve the village. Our customers, friends and neighbours had become very much part of our lives and we felt we would like as many of them as possible to join in this special occasion. We talked to our local vicar, Peter Hallett, who was very happy to incorporate the blessing in a normal church service the week after our civil ceremony. We therefore decided to hire the village hall for a couple of hours after the service and have an open-house "reception", to which all the village was invited. We organised a local caterer to provide pastries, coffee and sparkling wine and we put our open invitation in the Parish Magazine.

The day of our civil ceremony was a wonderful day with all our families and close friends present. One of my oldest friends was my matron of honour and Keith's son Richard was his best man. The ceremony was followed by dinner and dancing and a number of our guests joined us in staying the night at the hotel. On the Monday we took a couple of days off and drove down to Cornwall for a mini-honeymoon, thanks to our staff who took over the reins in the shop. On the following Sunday we walked up to our village church and found it packed out with all our friends and neighbours. The vicar commented that he wished we had a blessing every week to boost his congregation! The lady flower-arrangers at the church had decorated it beautifully and the choir from the village primary school, where Keith was Chair of Governors, sang during the service. At the end of the service, we left the church and found that the lych-gate had been tied up with white ribbon so that Keith had to lift me over for us to get out! On the other side of the gate there was a large crowd of villagers who showered us with confetti! We then walked down to the village hall where we were joined by over one hundred people who sipped champagne with us and wished us well. It really was very moving and quite overwhelming. What was equally humbling was that, unbeknown to us, Catherine had organised a collection for a wedding present for us from the village. We were presented with a wonderful signed card from everyone and a voucher for a considerable amount of money to be spent, at a local china shop, on the new dinner service we were trying to build up. One's wedding is always a memorable occasion but this was particularly special and was a week of amazing joy and friendship.

During our seven years in the shop, we were determined that we would achieve at least one break away per year and these breaks proved to be essential for us. Not only did we enjoy the change of scene and the lack of alarm clocks but we also worked on a number of the ideas which we had for the shop whilst our minds were clear of every-day routine tasks. Some of our holidays were taken overseas and some in this country and, somehow, each one had a twist which made it memorable. For instance, we flew to Majorca two days after 9/11! It was no doubt one of the safest times to fly but the horrors of 48 hours earlier were still in our minds as we queued at the airport and boarded the plane. It was also impossible not to look at the news every night for the week that we were away to check on the repercussions of this horrific attack and whether these might have implications for our homeward journey. We enjoyed the break but it was not the most relaxed that we have ever had.

On a much lighter note, two UK holidays come to mind as being memorable for other reasons. One spring, we decided to have a couple of nights in a country house hotel in the Lake District after visiting family in Yorkshire. The hotel was a beautiful old house in a stunning position overlooking Lake Windermere and the weather was dry but bitterly cold. The first problem that we encountered was that the heating was not working in our room and it was freezing. A complaint to reception produced a profuse apology and a couple of free-standing heaters and things started to improve. However, a decision to have a bath before changing for dinner uncovered another problem. There was some rather unpleasant-coloured water coming through the bathroom ceiling! Another complaint to reception produced further apologies and a transfer to another, much better room – and the heating worked! All went well until Keith started to pull the curtains on the enormous bay window overlooking the lake. One tug on the left-hand curtain brought it and the curtain rail tumbling down! We collapsed in hysterics and concluded that this shabby chic elegance was decidedly more shabby than chic!

The second holiday, which left a lasting impression, was at a hotel in Falmouth which we had chosen from its impressive brochure. Unfortunately, the reality did not live up to the publicity, except for the restaurant which was excellent. The general décor was dark wood, heavily patterned carpet, dark red flock wallpaper and bowls of faded artificial flowers. Our bedroom was similarly decorated and was dominated by an immense four-poster bed, around which it was just possible to squeeze. To say that we were disappointed would be an under-statement. However, the situation was somewhat redeemed by a good-sized bathroom with a new treat for us, a Jacuzzi bath. The first evening, I decided to try this out and I learnt an important lesson about Jacuzzi baths, do not put bubble bath in them. I was happily soaking up the warmth and steam until I pressed the button to activate the Jacuzzi. Within seconds I was disappearing in an ever-increasing mountain of bubbles and, by the time I managed to switch the Jacuzzi off, bubbles were streaming over the lip of the bath. I could not speak for laughing as Keith baled out the bathroom. At least my watery exploits had lightened our general mood and we went on to have an enjoyable week away.

Christmas

One of the times of the year that we particularly looked forward to and which we wanted to make special in the shop was Christmas. We started thinking about this even before we opened the shop and our first Christmas set the standard on which we built over the years. There were some products which we were happy to stock as they were either sure fire sellers or they had unlimited shelf life, like Christmas cards, but there were others that we felt were a bit risky but it would be good to be able to offer them. We then struck upon the idea of a Christmas Specialities List where customers would be given several weeks' notice of what we were going to stock and they would be able to place advance orders to ensure that they got what they wanted. This idea proved to be both popular and successful and over the years the List became ever more comprehensive. It also meant that we could minimise the amount of seasonal, time-limited stock we bought speculatively as most could be purchased to meet firm orders.

We eventually had a List covering four pages which included turkeys, joints of meat and ham, smoked salmon and gravalax, cheeses, Christmas cakes, Christmas puddings and other desserts, mince pies, jars of fruits in liqueurs, boxes and tins of chocolates and biscuits, clotted and double cream, fresh fruit and vegetables, Christmas trees and holly wreaths. Alongside this, Keith ran a Christmas-special beers, wines and spirits list which gave customers the opportunity to order either reduced price items or products in bulk. So popular did these arrangements become that people started asking for their lists earlier and earlier in order that they could be sure of getting what they wanted.

At our first Christmas, we only had Catherine working for us in the shop and, having taken innumerable orders for perishable goods, we needed extra help in putting all the orders together. On Christmas Eve, the ever-helpful Pam and Colin came down to give us assistance and Pam, Colin and I were positioned in what was a very cold back store with sacks of sprouts, potatoes, parsnips and carrots and boxes of every conceivable type of fruit, nuts and salad ingredients. The first thing which happened was that the spare scales which we had put in the store to weigh out the orders would not work. We had to resort to a set of scales with weights which was rather slow and not altogether accurate but I think our customers benefited because we tended to give them the benefit of the doubt! After about two hours of putting together orders, we were not quite so cold and we had a very satisfied feeling when we surveyed the lovely boxes of fruit and veg with which we were surrounded. It was always rather nerve-wracking being responsible for the bulk of our customers' Christmas food requirements and we checked and double checked the orders we had received to make sure we had not missed anything. I can honestly say that we never had anyone whose Christmas order was not fully satisfied and this presumably was the reason that our Specialities List arrangement was such a success.

As far as the shop itself was concerned, in early December we put up our Christmas decorations and everywhere became festooned in shiny gold and red chains and pendants. Fairy lights were placed around the inside of the windows and multi-coloured outside lights were draped across the whole of the shop-front. The decorations were completed with all the Christmas cards we received from our customers. In the last week before Christmas, we installed a "ghetto blaster" on top of one of the chill cabinets and had

Christmas carols playing throughout the day. The shelves were piled high with jars of fruits, mincemeat and pickles, the chill cabinets were full of stilton, brie, smoked salmon and joints of ham, boxes of Christmas crackers and fairy lights lined the tops of the shelves, packets of Christmas cards (including Village Shop Christmas cards which we designed ourselves for two years) were stacked six deep and big display boxes of wrapping paper were packed around the counter. The Post Office was heaving with bulging sacks of letters and parcels and queues of people lined up for their Christmas stamps whilst, outside, Christmas trees and holly wreaths leant up against the shop front.

We also organised two events around Christmas which we felt epitomised how we saw a village Christmas. Firstly, we invited the children from the village primary school to come down to the shop about two weeks before Christmas and sing Christmas carols outside the shop. This became a regular fixture in the school and village calendar and was much enjoyed by residents and parents alike. Being December, the weather was invariably cold but on no occasion did the event have to be called off. We did come close to it, however, one year when the local newspaper picked up on what we were doing and decided to send along a photographer. On this particular day it was bitterly cold and there had been snow flurries. The children bravely carried on and were roundly applauded for their efforts but there was no sign of the photographer. Not wishing to prolong their agony, we suggested that they gave up and went back to school. There they found the photographer who had gone to the wrong location. A stalwart half dozen or so children were sent back down to the shop to have their photograph taken which was completed in what was gradually becoming a blizzard!

We were very aware of the support that the adults were giving the children on these occasions and that standing outside a shop in December is not always pleasurable, however good the carol singing is. We therefore borrowed cups and saucers from the village hall and, as soon as the children started to arrive, we downed tools in the shop, except for helping the odd, persistent customer, and coffee and biscuits were delivered to the audience outside. This was much appreciated although we always had the odd person who required black coffee or who wanted more or less milk in theirs – despite the fact that they were being given it free! At the end of the carol singing we always had a tin of sweets ready for the children who had performed so well – and the teachers usually managed to pinch one or two for themselves!

The second event that became a tradition during our time in the shop was the Village Shop Christmas Party. We decided that we would like to show our customers our appreciation for their custom during the year as well as having a festive event in the shop, so we invited everyone to join us during the morning, usually on Christmas Eve, and we laid on wine, hot mince pies and various other nibbles such as small pork pies, crisps and biscuits. This was a much-appreciated start to the festive season which we continued during the seven years we had the shop and which our staff thoroughly enjoyed as well. The mainstay of our staffing for this event was John, Catherine's husband, who took on the role of barman for the morning and who served and entertained our customers royally. Father Christmas hats, flashing earrings and badges, illuminated bow ties and reindeer antlers were among the modes of dress we all adopted and which, by the time we closed at tea time on Christmas Eve, were in various states of collapse! That also describes how we felt when we had ensured that the final turkey had been collected, that the fridges were empty of ordered cream, cheese and desserts, that the last bags of sprouts and boxes of mince pies had been sold and that the glasses and dishes from the party had been washed up and the floor swept of crumbs. Tired but satisfied we were ready to start celebrating our own Christmas.

Some of The Boring Bits!

As with any business we had a certain amount of administration which had to be done and which was not always the most interesting or enjoyable part of our lives. Certain things had to be done daily, some weekly, some monthly and some annually as well as various ad hoc things which occurred from time to time. On a daily basis there was the checking of 'use by' and 'sell by' dates on produce. The former was more important than the latter as it was a statutory requirement not to sell any product over its 'use by' date. The 'sell by' date was an indication of when the quality of the product might start to deteriorate although it would not become a health hazard beyond that date. We soon became very frustrated with the way some products were dated. Obviously cooked and raw meat and fish products required very careful monitoring but sometime the dates on things like cooking fats and butter were much shorter than we knew the product would last but there was nothing we could do about it except either throw the item away – or eat it ourselves!

Tinned foods were another area where 'sell by' dates often seemed totally inappropriate. We were reminded of Polar expeditions where food had been found in tins, several decades later, entirely edible and we did have to wonder whether the dates on modern food were not more to do with marketing than health. The checking of tinned and packeted food on the shelves was a less regular occurrence than the chilled food. Obviously when we had our weekly delivery of stock from our wholesalers we put the new products behind the old ones on the shelves but somehow this system was not foolproof. About once a month we had a major cleaning exercise when we took products off the shelves, cleaned them, checked all the dates and put the items back on the shelves. Almost inevitably we found the goods out of date-order when we took them off the shelves. There was always one item, about three back in the line, which was older than everything in front of it. We put this down to either human error on our part, brought about by the sheer monotony of checking sometimes almost illegible dates on goods, or the foraging habits of our customers who dug around until they found a tin or whatever with a better date on it!

Apart from ensuring that we had a methodical turnover of stock and our customers had the best possible product choice, this process also had to be carried out to meet the requirements of Trading Standards. Their representatives could, and did, visit the shop unannounced and carry out a thorough inspection of all our stock on the shop floor and in the back stores. We had three or four inspections during our years in the shop and it never got less nerve wracking. The lady or gentleman would arrive with briefcase and clipboard, introduce themselves and announce that they were going to carry out an inspection. We would smile confidently and invite them to carry on whilst keeping everything crossed that we had not missed anything. When the inspector was delving into the bottom of the chest freezer we would realise that, whilst we did check the dates of everything in there, because it was such a cold and unpleasant job, we probably had not done a recent check. Visions of severely over-date fish fingers loomed before our eyes together with a loud announcement from the inspector to this effect in front of a shop full of customers who rapidly departed never to return again! Luckily this nightmare never materialised and we were given a clean bill of health on every occasion.

Our major stock exercise every year was our annual stock-take which we carried out at the end of March to coincide with the end of our financial year. This involved counting and listing every item of stock and then tabulating the totals under the various stock headings which we had on the till, e.g. food, non-food, cigarettes, alcohol, stationery etc. We took the decision not to close during this process but the ever-willing John, Catherine's husband, would come down to help Keith, Catherine, me and whoever else was also employed by us at the time. It would take five of us, with one of us manning the counter as necessary, around 4 hours to count all the stock in the shop, in two back stores and in the loft over the shop. It was a rather mind-numbing process but, given the participants, it often ended up becoming hilarious with people losing count because they were laughing so much. The one area where we drew the line at actual counting was the confectionery counter. There was no way we were going to accurately count all the Mars Bars, Fruit Pastilles and Kitkats. We used to count how many were in a row, how many it was deep and multiply the two together. Not very scientific but we worked on the principle that nobody was going to check us! When we finished at lunchtime and we closed the shop at 1.30 p.m., we would take our helpers either next door to the pub or into the cottage for lunch and a bottle of wine, which at least rounded the counting process off on a high. My next job, over the following week or so, was to add up all the figures. There was sheet upon sheet of twelve times this tin at 95p and 15 times that packet at £1.05 which then had to be finally totalled. This was a tedious job but in the end it was always interesting to be able to compare from one year to the next the value of the stock we were holding and the mix of products we were selling.

Another tedious job, at least I thought so, was compiling the annual accounts and the quarterly VAT returns but luckily Keith had accounting experience and enjoyed figure work, although even he had a love/hate relationship with the VAT returns. From the very start of our trading, Keith had maintained the sales and expenditure ledgers which was often a Sunday morning job. Sunday morning in the shop could be quite busy but, once we had put the newspapers together, there were no deliveries, no Post Office and only a couple of orders to fax or transmit to suppliers so, in relative terms, it was a quieter time for us. We fell into a routine of me doing various cleaning jobs in the shop whilst Keith served at the counter and, in between times, he sat at the Post Office desk and completed the week's figures. At one stage we decided that we really ought to enter the 20th century and invest in a computerised accounting system. This was not a success! Firstly, the software we bought, based on the advice we had received, did not suit the type of business we ran. It assumed that the business issued a lot of invoices as well as paying a lot of bills. The latter was true of the shop but the former was largely irrelevant for a convenience store. Secondly, with our limited computer experience the system seemed complicated and appeared to have a lot of quirks which we had neither the time nor the inclination to master. So, we abandoned technology and Keith reverted to the tried and tested method of manual book-keeping.

Life became more interesting when we reached the end of our financial year and the first pass at the accounts had to be made before the books were passed to our accountant. This exercise had to be done in the relative quiet of the cottage and Keith would take all the relevant paperwork into the kitchen, together with a rather ancient calculator with a paper roll, and set about trying to reconcile all the figures. This he always achieved but usually only after we had both sat, head in hands, trying to spot an error or a mis-keying on the calculator. The kitchen would be strewn with screwed up pieces of paper, metres of calculator roll and sheaves of receipts and invoices. Once Keith was satisfied that he had done as much as possible of this work, it was all bundled up and sent to our accountant who then, after a few weeks, came back with a range of queries and questions which once again tested our memories. Eventually the accounts would be signed off, the paperwork would be boxed up and put in the loft, never to be looked at again, and the whole process would start its annual cycle once more.

Keith's daughter and son-in-law, Liam and Allison Kennedy, and his mother, May, at Bramble Cottage

Four generations of the Gudgeon family – l. to r. Richard, William, May and Keith

William Gudgeon and Gertie "Dyson" taking the air outside the shop !

Sue and her son, Richard Browning, at St. James' Palace when Richard received his Gold Duke of Edinburgh's Award

Charlton Horethorne C. of E. Primary School Choir who sang at the blessing of Sue and Keith's marriage

Sue and Keith attempting to leave the church of St. Peter and St. Paul, Charlton Horethorne, after the blessing of their marriage, through decorations put in place by the villagers !

The children of Charlton Horethorne C. of E. Primary School singing Christmas carols outside The Village Shop

Bill Closs and Catherine Matthew enjoying The Village Shop Christmas party

New Services

We were always on the lookout for new services which we could provide to our customers and sometimes they would suggest things to us – not that we always took them up on all their suggestions! One service that we had wanted to provide from the start was the provision of Calor Gas cylinders. As I mentioned earlier, the village has never had a mains gas supply and some people used Calor Gas as a means of cooking and heating. In addition, there was a summer trade for those with caravans who used the small cylinders whilst on holiday. We could not start stocking the cylinders until the building work on the cottage was completed as they had to be stored a certain distance from the shop, for safety reasons, and this meant putting them in the back garden by the garage. The purchase of a gas cylinder is unlike any other purchase in that the customer has to enter into an agreement with Calor Gas to hire the cylinder which, when it is empty, can then be exchanged for a full one. We would call the supplier with an order which would be delivered to the shop and he would then remove the empty cylinders and take them back to the depot to be refilled. There was only one problem with this service and that was the weight of the cylinders. The large, full, 9 Kg ones were extremely heavy. Keith could lift them relatively easily but even he found heaving one into the boot of an elderly customer's car pretty strenuous. This was aggravated when he was asked to deliver a cylinder to an elderly or infirm customer who then wanted it positioned in the house in usually a particularly awkward location. Similarly, I would dread it if, when I was working on my own in the shop in the afternoon, for instance, a customer drew up outside and proceeded to unload an empty cylinder. If Keith was out I had one of two choices. Either I could ask the customer to come out through the back of the shop and into our garden to collect his own cylinder, with all the security implications that exposed, or I could manhandle the cylinder myself. This involved inching it along the path, down four steps, up one step, over a door surround and into the back of the shop. It could take me a good five minutes to complete this exercise and it meant that I left the shop unmanned for the period I was grappling with the cylinder. Usually, the customer concerned was known to us and I therefore took the easy option and sent them out into the garden to collect their own cylinder but I was always glad when Keith returned and I did not have this difficult choice to make.

On the subject of heating, we were surprised when we approached our first winter in the shop to find that we were being asked for kindling wood. Coming from the South East where the norm was central heating or coal- or wood-effect gas fires, we had not anticipated that so many people would either rely upon or choose to have open fires as a regular source of heat and would therefore require kindling wood. We set about trying to find a supplier for this and hit upon a source which was not only reliable but which also helped another part of the community. There was a day-centre in Sherborne for mentally handicapped people which ran a workshop producing a number of wooden products which they sold to help fund the centre. As a result of this production, they had a lot of off-cuts which they bundled and sold for kindling wood and they became our regular suppliers. This was certainly a case of a local initiative benefiting all parties.

Living in the country has a lot of attractions, not least of which is the range of wild life which one comes across, particularly wild birds. We had wrongly thought that most of the wild birds living in the country would be self-sufficient and that country folk would see them as such but we were wrong on both counts. Like their counterparts in the town, birds in the country need their diets supplemented, particularly in the winter, and the vast majority of our customers were keen to help feed them. As a consequence we were soon asked for wild bird food and again we went on the hunt for a supplier. Luckily, there is an amazingly well-stocked outlet, called Crossroads, housed in a rather basic and very chilly single storey building on the dual-carriageway between Sherborne and Yeovil. This supplier was happy to sell to us in bulk and give us a discount but we had to buy wild bird seed and peanuts by the sack full and this meant at least monthly trips with the car to stock up. When we got back to the shop we then opened the sacks and positioned them near the till and equipped them with scoops so that bags could be filled with the quantity each customer requested. This was a mistake. There were two ways of filling the bags, either directly over the sack, in which case all the overflow ended up on the shop floor or in between the sweets on the confectionery counter, or we scooped the seed directly onto the scales and then poured it into bags, in which case all the surplus ended up on the floor behind the counter and in amongst the keys on the till. We thought we had solved this problem when we started to bag up half and one kilo bags ready for sale. At least we could do the bagging up at our leisure and not when we were under pressure with customers at the counter and we would therefore end up with less mess dispersed around the shop. Wrong again! The bags we used were plastic bags we supplied to our customers to put their fruit and vegetables in and whilst they were ideal for this purpose they were not very strong. We soon found that our pre-packed bags of seed and peanuts were being picked up by customers, put in the wire shopping baskets which we provided and, in doing so, the bags were snagging on the sharp edges of the wire. The customer could then be traced around the shop by the trail of bird seed they were leaving in their wake! We also had customers who brought their own containers, be they bags, jars or tins, and asked for them to be filled with seed or peanuts. Most people were quite relaxed about having their container filled, weighed and then paying the resulting cost. There was, however, one customer who insisted on having her plastic carrier bag weighed before being filled and the negligible weight deducted from the price of her purchase! We concluded, in the end, that there was no ideal way to sell this commodity and we opted for a combination of all three methods!

When we first opened we provided a film developing service via one of the companies who supply pre-paid envelopes into which customers put their films and post them to the developer. The deal was that we got a small percentage for every envelope which emanated from our shop. Whilst this was at least a basic service it did not provide people with the chance to have reprints done or enlargements or any of the other special services you normally get from a photographic developer. We hunted around and found a company in Wells who were prepared to provide this service and it proved to be quite popular, particularly before the advent of digital cameras and computer downloading. The service had been ticking over quite nicely when we had a visit from one of the directors of the company who happened to be in the area. He had decided to call in to meet us face to face and confirm that we were happy with the service his company was providing. During the course of this conversation, the gentleman concerned asked whether a certain lady still lived in the village as he had worked with her husband before he had died. When we confirmed that she was still a resident, our visitor asked whereabouts she lived as he would like to call on her. As he was known to us, we could not see any reason why we should not tell him and he left the shop to drive to the lady's house to renew his acquaintance. The following day the lady concerned came in and, although she was not cross with us, she did ask that we did not send her any more gentlemen callers! She said that she had known him as a colleague of her late husband's and she had not liked him that much then and she certainly did not want him calling on her now! That was the last time we played the role of Friends Reunited!

Another of the services we introduced in our first year was that of video rental. DVD's had not hit the market at that stage and the main source of entertainment was still video rental. We engaged the services of a company called Crazy Eddy's who supplied the initial video rental stock together with a display stand. A certain number of videos were then exchanged each month, via the postal service, to keep the selection current. I think we should have guessed by their business name that our relationship with Crazy Eddy's would not last too long! The promised choice of films became more and more limited and obscure and eventually we changed suppliers in 1998 to In Store Movies. This proved to be a much better service with a representative calling with a van every six weeks or so and changing about 20% of the videos for new ones. We could also pay extra for particularly popular new films or order specific films for customers, which was a far better arrangement. Apart from the usual family and children's film rental, which was the main core of the business, we also had what could only be described as 'top shelf' films and we had one or two amusing moments with the rental of these. There was one very quiet married man, who sometimes shopped on other occasions with his two children, who frequently called in after work and rented a 'top shelf' film on his way home. He came unstuck, however, on one occasion when he returned a video to us, which he had rented elsewhere, presumably returning our video to the other outlet. We decided that we should be discreet and not contact him at home and so we waited for him to come in the next time and pointed out the mistake. He appeared totally unabashed and sorted out the error with the other supplier. Another of our 'top shelf' customers was a charming retired gentleman whose wife quite regularly went away with friends. On these occasions, he would come into the shop, buy the most expensive ready-meals available, purchase a large bottle of Scotch and rent a 'top shelf' video. We never knew if his wife knew of his activities in her absence.

One other service, or I suppose you could call it a product, which we provided in our first two years in the shop was the provision of fireworks for Bonfire Night. This required us to acquire and pay for a licence and to have a lockable cabinet in which the fireworks were stored at all times. We went into this in our first year thinking that it would be a popular extra service and, to some extent, it was but the minimum quantity of fireworks we had to buy was quite large and we had stock left after the first November. Storing these was a bit of a problem but we had inherited a steel box with a lid on it in the loft over the shop so we packed our surplus away in this. During the next year we reviewed our decision to sell fireworks in the light of our first year's experience and we decided that we would just sell off our surplus and we would not offer them for sale after that. The trend was very much towards public displays rather than private firework parties and, as there was an excellent event already being run in the village, we did not see any benefit in our continuing to sell these very risky products. The stock that was left after our second year's sales was donated to the village event and we were pleased to see the back of them.

The Good, the Bad and the Sad

Whilst the vast majority of our customers were pleasant, friendly and a pleasure to deal with, we did have occasions when we could not quite believe what we were seeing or having to deal with. Probably the first example of this happened quite shortly after we opened. A lady came into the shop, looked around and then came to the counter carrying a jar of marmalade. The jar was the type with a screw-on lid which had, in the centre, a vacuum seal which ensured that the jar had not been opened or tampered with. The lady put the jar on the counter and, pointing to the seal, said to me "I always have trouble opening these type of lids. Can you help me?"

The customer was probably in her seventies and I assumed that she probably had some sort of arthritis in her wrists. So I called Keith over and said "Could you help this lady with this jar. She has trouble opening the lid."

Keith duly opened the jar and showed her how the vacuum device worked. The lady then expressed her profuse thanks – and walked out! She never bought anything and we were left at the counter with mouths and a jar of marmalade well and truly open!

Later in our time at the shop we started to stock pre-packed fresh meat from a local butcher who would also take orders for larger joints and special cuts of meat, but more about this later. On one particular occasion, a lady who shopped with us on a rather ad hoc basis came in and ordered a leg of lamb. This particular lady was also probably in her seventies and was very well spoken and always immaculately dressed and made up. She gave the impression of having lived abroad with her husband in circumstances where she probably had staff. Although she was very friendly she always appeared rather out of place doing any food shopping. When she called for her leg of lamb she appeared to be delighted and left the shop on the Friday afternoon with what we had assumed she was going to be cooking on Sunday. On the following Thursday we had a telephone call from her saying that she had a problem with the leg of lamb which we had sold her. Keith took the call and apologised for any dissatisfaction she had experienced and asked her to describe what had gone wrong. The bottom line was that she still had not cooked the lamb and, one week on, she was complaining that it had gone off! It took all Keith's diplomatic skills to explain to her that fresh meat had a shelf life of slightly less than a week!

Without wishing to blow our own trumpets, we soon became aware that the village was delighted and proud to have a thriving village shop back in operation and it was a common occurrence for family and friends to be brought into the shop by residents to show them what we had done. This was lovely and usually the visitors purchased several items to take home with them. There was, however, one resident whose only regular purchase from us was her daily paper but who also liked to bring her friends and family to the shop when they were visiting. The big difference here was that they were shown around as though they were visiting a local monument and comments were made in our hearing which were tactless to say the least. The worst example of this was when, on one occasion, a friend of this resident actually came to the counter with a purchase only to be told by her hostess "You don't want to buy that here. We can get it much cheaper in Sherborne!"

To her credit, the visitor flushed red and looked very embarrassed but she was chaperoned away without her purchase. It would appear that some people feel that they can say anything in front of a shopkeeper because, in some way, the counter between you makes you devoid of any feelings.

The apparent dulling of your senses also seems to extend to basic hygiene as far as some customers are concerned. At one time there was a family from London who had a house in the village and they used to descend at weekends and in school holidays with two small children and a nanny in tow. They were reasonably good customers when they came down but it soon became obvious that the wife, who had some high-powered job in the City, was the driving force in the family and she carried over some of her managerial style when dealing with us in the shop. Our one main problem with her was her laundry. The dry cleaning service which we offered also had a laundry service which she used regularly including, we think, bringing her washing from London! We did not mind this at all, it was good business, but what we did object to was when she came into the shop on a busy Saturday morning and start to deposit all her dirty sheets straight onto the counter. She brought them all down in black bags but insisted on taking her bags back with her. This meant that we were left to put her dirty sheets in containers as quickly as we could so that we could get them away from the bread and cakes and other food items around the counter. It was not with a great feeling of disappointment that we heard that they were moving to a neighbouring village and taking their dirty washing with them!

Someone else who moved out of the village whilst we owned the shop was an elderly gentleman who fell foul of a scam which we could see coming but about which it was impossible to warn him. Impossible because, firstly, he would have accused us of interfering and, secondly, he would not have believed us. The gentleman concerned was selling his house and moving to somewhere smaller and he had a quantity of silver which he wanted to dispose of. He came into the shop one day looking very pleased with himself because he had contacted someone who was advertising her interest in buying silver and this lady was coming to see him. He was particularly keen to meet her as, being an ex-Army man himself, she had told him that she had a brother in the Army. This obviously increased her credibility in his eyes, although we can only assume that she had told him this after he had let slip what his background was. In any event, the lady came to his house and he was much taken with her, and she with his silver. She gave him a price, which he found acceptable, and he allowed her to leave with his silver on the promise of a forthcoming cheque. Needless to say the cheque never arrived. This was a very sad episode in this gentleman's life, particularly at a time when he was moving out of a house in which he and his wife had lived for many years.

There were occasions when we were put in a difficult position by customers who either told us things or involved us in matters which we had to keep confidential, sometimes against our better judgement. The first occasion once again involved the unfortunate gentleman who was conned out of his precious silver. Some time after this event he finally sold his house and moved to another village about ten miles away. However, he still had friends in Charlton Horethorne and came back at least once or twice a week and he usually dropped into the shop either for some small purchase or for a chat with Keith. They were both ardent cricket fans and enjoyed a lively banter about the relative merits of various county cricket clubs and their players. During one of these conversations, the gentleman concerned mentioned that he had just been up to his old house, which was now occupied by the purchasers, and he commented that he did not particularly like what they had done to the property. We assumed that he had been invited back by the new owners but it then transpired that he still had a key to the house and, as they were living some of the time in London at this stage, he had let himself in and had a look around! We were stunned and speechless and at a loss to know what to do. In the event, we did nothing as there was no reason to believe the gentleman would do any harm to the property or its contents but we felt very uncomfortable about being party to this knowledge.

Another very difficult situation occurred when an elderly lady customer of ours asked us to look after her bank books when she went into hospital. This particular lady was very well thought of in the village and, in fact, the village had nominated her for a national award which she had travelled to Buckingham Palace to receive from the Queen a couple of years before we came to Charlton Horethorne. She was a small lady who, sadly, had a very unhappy home life and helping other people was not only in her nature but it also gave her a purpose in life. Despite her stature she was full of life and probably came into the shop two or three times a day as well as making one or two trips to the pub every day for her Guinness! Both these activities were also ways of getting her out of the house and filling her day. Unfortunately she became ill and had to go into hospital. Just before she went in she came in to see us and asked us to take care of her paying in books and so on because she did not want to leave them in the house in case her husband got hold of them. We felt a little uncomfortable about this but, knowing her circumstances, we took the books and put them in our safe. Sadly the lady concerned died within a week or so of going into hospital and we were now left in the awkward position of having to give her banking information back to her husband. This we did and luckily he did not make an issue out of why we had been given them in the first place. We felt honoured that she had trusted us with the responsibility but also very sad that their relationship was such that she felt she had to do it at all.

One incident that was both poignant and comical occurred after we had been in the shop several years. I was looking after the shop one afternoon and it was relatively quiet with just a couple of customers browsing around when a police car drove up and parked outside. A policeman got out of the car, walked into the shop and came up to me at the counter. "Are you the owner of the shop?" he asked.

"One of them," I answered. "Why?"

"We have had a report that you have got a dead body in the shop," he said. I was stunned and then I saw the funny side of it.

"Well," I said, "Those customers over there still look alright and there does not seem to be a funny smell coming from anywhere so I don't think we have any dead bodies. You can check the freezer if you like!"

The policeman smiled and said that that would not be necessary. The police had not really thought that the call that they had received was a serious one but that they thought that they should check it out, just in case. With that, he left. The customers in the shop had heard all this going on and were highly amused but the whole incident left Keith and me puzzled as to how it had been initiated in the first place.

The mystery was solved shortly afterwards and turned out to be rather sad. A gentleman who, with his late wife, had previously run the shop for a number of years as a tenant of the owners Mr. and Mrs. Peacock, had fairly recently gone into a care home. He was in a rather confused state but he was still able to walk to nearby shops in the town in which he was living. One afternoon he had left his room in the care home to go into town and he had walked past a neighbouring room. The lady occupant of the room was lying on the floor as she had a bad back. It was her habit to lay on the floor in the afternoons to get some respite from the discomfort. Our gentleman had seen her there and, in his confused state, had visualised that he was back running the shop in Charlton Horethorne. He concluded that something dreadful had happened and he went straight out to the nearest telephone box and called the police to tell them that there was a body on the floor of the shop! Hence the visit from our friendly neighbourhood policeman. All rather sad but also, at the time, quite amusing.

During our time in the shop we also had two villagers go missing. The first one was an elderly gentleman who, we had noticed, had been getting progressively more vague and confused on his visits up to the shop but we did not realise how serious this was. One morning he came up for his newspaper as usual and we did not think any more about it until his wife rang approximately an hour later and asked if we had seen him. When we told her that he had left some time ago, she thanked us and put the telephone down. We later learnt that he had got in his car to drive the quarter of a mile home but did not arrive and he was subsequently found in Wiltshire, 30 or so miles away, not knowing where he was or why he was there. This was obviously very disturbing for his wife and it was ultimately the start of a serious deterioration in his health.

The second person to go missing caused quite a stir but was luckily found safe and well. The lady in question suddenly disappeared from home, which was quite out of character, and this caused her husband and children a great deal of distress and anxiety. They eventually called the police and a full scale search was instigated. A police incident room was set up in the skittle alley in the pub next door and teams of police with dogs started combing the area. Various residents offered to help in search parties but the police kept these offers at arms length in the early stages whilst they used their specialist teams. Needless to say theories abounded about what had happened to her and they ranged from the farcical to the gruesome. After several days, happily the lady was eventually found fit and well in Wiltshire. The excitement of a major police search soon evaporated and the village returned to normal, relieved that there had been a successful outcome to what had seemed, at one time, a very serious situation.

Whenever possible we liked to help people but sometimes our generosity came back to bite us. One afternoon a car pulled up outside the shop and an older lady came in and asked if there were any public toilets in the village. This was a question we were quite often asked and nine times out of ten we just replied in the negative and directed people to the nearest town which was ten minutes away. When I gave this response on this particular afternoon, the lady pleaded with me that she and her friend had an elderly lady in her nineties in the car and they did not think they could make it into town. Please could I help? I weakened and offered them the use of the staff toilet at the back of the shop. The elderly lady and one of her companions went through to the toilet whilst the third member of the party stayed in the shop and at least did the decent thing and did a little shopping. When the two ladies emerged from the back of the shop, they thanked me profusely and said that it was just as well that I had been able to help as the elderly lady had had "an accident". Too much information, I thought, as I watched them leave. Little did I know, until I went into the back of the shop, quite what they meant. Without going into graphic details, the results of the "accident" had been left on the floor of our toilet! I then spent half an hour with rubber gloves and disinfectant cleaning up and vowing never to be soft hearted again!

Our help was much more appreciated, however, one Sunday when we had a telephone call from a very agitated lady who was one of our regular customers. A gentleman who lived in the village and who was an old friend of hers had been up to have a pre-lunch drink with her. This gentleman had been having some health problems which seemed to affect his balance and whether this was the problem on this occasion or whether it was the strength of the gins and tonics we never knew. Anyhow, when the gentleman got up leave he had tripped and fallen on the lady's drive and hit his head. He was conscious but he could not get up and the lady, being riddled with arthritis and only about five foot tall, was in no position to help. She had therefore telephoned us to see if Keith could go up to her house and assist. This particular weekend we had my stepdaughter, Allison, and her husband, Liam, staying and we were just about to sit down to Sunday lunch. Keith was wary of trying to attempt to lift this gentleman on his own so Liam went with him, which was very brave because Liam cannot stand the sight of blood! The outcome was that Keith and Liam managed to get the gentleman sat up, got a cloth to hold to the nasty gash on the back of his head and waited for the ambulance to arrive. Eventually they both came back to the cottage and I was able to dish up the Sunday lunch although, strangely, Liam did not seem to have too much of an appetite!

Post Office

We had always viewed the Post Office as a sprat to catch a mackerel when we opened the shop, on the basis that customers had to come in for their pensions, child benefit, disability benefit, stamps and other postal services and therefore they were all potential customers for the shop. I think we were right in this assumption because to have had a village shop without a Post Office would have been a much bigger uphill struggle but from the beginning the revenue from the shop far exceeded the earnings from the Post Office. In latter years, with the removal of cash payment of pensions and child allowance, the removal of television licences and other reductions in the range of services provided by the Post Office, the argument for a village shop always having a Post Office is much diminished.

I have given something of the flavour of work in the Post Office in my description of life leading up to and immediately after opening in July 1996 but there were various incidents which occurred over the next seven years which stand out from the general day to day business and mind-numbing administration. I referred earlier to the antiquated date stamp which we inherited from the Post Office and the fact that we had to purchase our own up-to-date, automatic stamp ourselves. What I did not mention was the unexpected visitation we had because of this change. We had a visit from the official Post Office historian! We had no idea that such a person existed but he rang up one day and asked if he could visit because he had heard that we were changing the date stamp. We were rather bemused by this request but agreed to him coming and on the day a gentleman arrived at the shop looking just like one would expect a Post Office historian to look. He was a man in his forties with a profusion of curly dark hair, a beard and glasses and he wore a checked shirt and a tweed jacket over twill trousers and hefty Hush-Puppy type shoes. He was very affable and an enormous enthusiast and regaled us with many stories of the history of the Post Office. The purpose of his visit was to take the last date stamp of the old Post Office stamp before it was superseded by the new one and then remove the old one to be placed in some dusty vaults somewhere in the Post Office archives. To be perfectly honest the significance of all this left us somewhat cold but we were happy to go along with it to oil the wheels of Post Office history.

Another visitor to the Post Office was not quite so welcome and that was the Post Office auditor. Over the years we had a number of visits from the auditor and they were always a nerve-wracking experience. Like the inspections by Trading Standards, the Post Office auditors always arrived unannounced, usually at about 8.00 a.m. and the purpose of the exercise was to check all the money and stock that we were holding to ensure that it tallied with the figures which we had produced on the last weekly balance. If all went well, the audit would be completed by the time we were due to open the Post Office at 8.30 a.m., if not, we would still be scrabbling through paperwork, stamps and cash when our first customer arrived. Luckily this very seldom occurred and we were always given a clean bill of health even if sometimes we only completed the audit just as we were due to open.

In general, our relationship with the Post Office hierarchy was polite and usually distant but occasionally we had disagreements with them and on one occasion this became quite acrimonious. One principle by which the Post Office seemed to work was that, if an error occurred, it was always the fault of the Sub Postmaster – you were presumed guilty until proved innocent. This was at best annoying and at worst insulting and aggravated us intensely because it seemed to be a case of the minnow versus the whale. In a Sub Post Office, it is the responsibility of the Sub Postmaster to order cash if he or she thinks the Office will run short during the week and equally he or she must return excess cash if, for instance, a significant amount has been paid in that week. The money is delivered and collected on a weekly basis by a security van. The notes are bundled into standard amounts and the coins are bagged in standard quantities in plastic bags. This money is then checked to ensure the stated amount has been delivered before it is stowed in the safe. Similarly, the money which is going to be sent back to the Post Office is checked on site before it is despatched and we had a system whereby at least two of us checked the amounts to ensure that we were accurate in what we were despatching. Our major fall-out with the Post Office came over some money we had sent back. One day we had a telephone call from the receiving depot to say that they were £100 short on a return of cash, which they had received from us, and that we would have to make up the shortfall. There was no discussion, no indication of any investigation, no acceptance that there could have been an error at their end, it was our fault and that was all there was to it. Needless to say, we were not happy because we were absolutely certain that we had sent the correct amount back. Various accusatory phone calls went on between us with Keith, who had by now taken over the battle on my behalf, demanding to speak to ever-more senior managers at each stage of the disagreement. In the end the Post Office agreed to waive the request for reimbursement but this still felt like a concession on their part rather than an acceptance of our innocence. We never quite got used to the feeling that we were not trusted.

The major piece of administration that we had to complete weekly was the balance on a Wednesday afternoon. Every week I had to balance the stock against the business that had been conducted during the week and if I had any surpluses or shortfalls I had to track down why and rectify them. Whilst in theory this should have balanced to the penny every week, it never did and I was told by every other Sub Postmaster that theirs never did either! Given the volume and variety of the business and the enormity of the stock of stamps, postal orders and cash, it was very easy to miscount something. Unofficially, the Post Office turned a blind eye to small surpluses or shortfalls because it was really not worth the Sub Postmaster's time trying to track down the last £20 in a weekly business turning over around £10,000. However there were times when I did the first balance and it was wildly out. I then had the stomach-churning fear that something major had gone wrong but I tried to remain calm whilst I re-counted everything and checked all my entries. I usually carried out this procedure sat at the Post Office counter, which was fine because the Post Office was not open in the afternoons. This fact, however, was lost on a lot of our customers for the whole time we owned the shop and my concentration was not helped by people peering over the 'Closed' sign and pushing their post under the screen for stamping. When I still could not find the mistake I had made, I used to call for Keith and he took over checking what I had done. Nine times out of ten it was a simple mistake like putting figures in the wrong column, adding them up wrong or miscounting a bundle of twenty pound notes! I was never more pleased than when we had completed the figures, put all the paperwork in the brown pouch for despatch the following morning and finished the whole exercise for another week!

This was not, however, necessarily the end of the matter. Envelopes would arrive in the post with the dreaded 'Error Notices' in them. These referred to errors which had been detected in our balances but the problem was that these Notices usually related to business conducted up to 8 weeks previously. Tracking back what we had done wrong, particularly when there was such a time delay and it could have been any one of three of us who worked in the Post Office, was a nightmare. In the days when pensioners were still receiving their pensions in cash, it was quite possible to stamp their books and forget to take the docket out when you paid their pension. We would then get a notice of a pension paid for which there was no documentary evidence. There would then be a group scratching of heads to try and work out which of our pensioners received that particular amount of pension and then we would carefully check their books when they came in to try and spot the error. On one occasion, one of our pensioners even rang us up after she had been in to collect her money to say that she had noticed that we had not removed the dockets from her book! That brought a whole new meaning to customer care!

The biggest change to our operation of the Post Office came when Post Office Counters Ltd. introduced a national computer system called Horizon in 2000. This meant that every Post Office in the country would have a computer terminal through which it would conduct its business and carry out its administration. There were all shades of opinion throughout the Post Office community, from the little old lady who had been doing the job for forty years and could not conceive of doing it any other way, let alone via a computer, to those of us who had worked in computerised environments and welcomed any innovation which would make the job easier. At this time, Sue was working for us in the Post Office and she was very apprehensive about working with a computer but, to give her her due, she embraced the training with enthusiasm and was soon a convert when we went live. Before that, however, we had a number of visits from various technicians who set up the workstations for us, put in the wiring and tested all the kit. They had various stories to tell which underlined the diversity of the Post Office empire and the complexity of installing such a national system. The engineers were carrying out installations throughout the UK, from the Scottish Highlands and islands down to the Scilly Isles, and the locations they encountered were many and various. At one site, they had entered what was, to all intents and purposes, a small cottage and the Post Office was run from the lady's front room. She had a small counter in one corner which, when she was not busy, doubled as her ironing board and on the day the installers arrived she was engrossed in the family laundry! Security was also an issue because of the expensive kit which was being installed and the technicians were concerned in one small hamlet to find that there was no security at the cottage Post Office at all. The lady involved pointed out, however, that her husband was a part-time Police Officer and that when he was not at home she hung his helmet by the door. In her view, that was security enough!

Once all our kit was installed, we were not allowed to go live until both Sue and I had been on a two-day training course and passed an exam. Sue and I were ladies of a certain age who probably had not taken an exam for 25 years and we were therefore rather apprehensive. However, we need not have worried. The course was very comprehensive and, without wishing to demean our fellow students, did cover a lot of basic information.

The exam was computer based and we each had our own terminal to work through various exercises at our own pace and therefore it was not particularly stressful. At the end of the whole process we were both given a certificate of competence which we had to produce to the technician who came to activate our system. Once we had got used to finding our way around the system we found it to be an enormous improvement and it made doing the weekly balance one hundred times easier. I think, in general, all Post Offices eventually embraced the new technology with enthusiasm although the stories in the press of parish councils supporting little old lady Sub Postmistresses who were being "driven out" by the Post Office rumbled on for several months. As far as we were concerned it was definitely a step in the right direction.

Another step in the right direction, although on nothing like the scale of the Horizon system, was the introduction of self-adhesive stamps. Now you would have thought that our customers would have been delighted not having to lick their stamps any more, particularly when they moaned and groaned about the taste and made veiled hints that the glue could be detrimental to their health. But, oh no! As soon as the self-adhesive stamps were introduced the complaints started. They could not get them off the backing, they were too fiddly, they could easily be peeled off letters etc. etc. It only went to prove that you cannot please all the people all the time! From our point of view, given that we stuck an awful lot of stamps on parcels etc. which customers left with us, we could not have been more pleased. We were just disappointed that it was only the first and second class stamps that had this facility, all the other denominations still had to be licked! This was overcome when the Horizon system developed a method of printing self-adhesive labels indicating the postage which had been paid. Once again customers complained that their relations overseas, in particular, wanted pretty stamps and not printed labels so we reverted to stamps for these items. We also had problems with some items of post when we had printed the label. When we went to stick it on, we found that the customer had left insufficient space on the envelope for a large, white, sticky label! We ended up wrapping it over the top, round the edges, any way to show that the postage had been paid! This was usually done after the customer had left the shop – what the eye did not see, the heart could not grieve over!

Inevitably, we had post to despatch for our customers to all corners of the world, particularly at Christmas time, but there were some occasions when these despatches were more interesting than others. When we first moved to the village, there was a young family living up the road from us and the husband was a talented sculptor. Peter Robinson's work was apparently known world-wide and we were very impressed when, one day, he came into the Post Office to despatch some drawings and a quotation to the American tycoon, Donald Trump. There was a certain incongruity between the office of despatch and the office of receipt which we found quite amusing!

We also became involved in the despatch of mail to HM forces as there were several families in the vicinity whose sons or husbands were serving overseas. This became particularly evident during the invasion of Iraq when the younger son of one our neighbours was serving as a Royal Marine based in Basra. It was obviously a very worrying time for his parents and they wrote to him regularly. On one occasion, with his mother's approval, we wrote a good luck message to him on the back of her envelope before we sent it off. As a result, when he thankfully returned safely, his parents invited us to an amazing welcome-home party which they held for him in a magnificent barn on their farm. It was a very happy and emotional occasion at which copious amounts of an amazing hog-roast were eaten, washed down with liberal quantities of alcohol!

Although we did not employ them, the other significant members of the Post Office team were the postmen with whom we had daily contact. They delivered the post to us in the morning and then returned at the end of their deliveries to collect the mail that we had accumulated in the Post Office. This process was repeated in the afternoon, when they collected from the post boxes in the neighbourhood and did a final collection from us, at around 4.30 p.m. This routine changed at the weekend, when they called only once on Saturday morning and again on Sunday morning when they just emptied the letter-box in the wall outside the shop.

This latter collection was a contentious area. The box outside the shop was a small, antique one set into the wall and it had quite a narrow opening into which letters were posted. This meant that if customers had anything to post, which was larger than a normal letter, they would bring it into us to put in the post sack. The Sunday postmen were divided into two camps, those who would willingly take any post we were holding and those who would not take it from us on a Sunday at any price. So vehement were some of these postmen in their refusal to take mail from us, that they would park their vans out of sight so that, by the time we realised that they had collected from the box, it was too late to catch them before they drove off. On one occasion, I pursued the postman with some letters, which I knew were particularly urgent and, to avoid taking them, he roared off in his van at such speed that he nearly ran me over!

This paints a picture of our postmen which is, largely, unfair as the vast majority of them were very helpful and pleasant. Outstanding amongst them was Mark, a dark-haired, cheery, young man in his thirties and Gary, who was about the same age, had a beard and shoulder-length hair, wore shorts for the majority of the year and was always cheerful and helpful. However, our regular postman, Dave Sneade, was almost a legend in his own time. Dave knew everyone in the village, elderly and children alike, and had a routine of breakfast and cups of tea at various houses in the village as he carried out his round. He would bring letters down to the Post Office, for house-bound residents, and use the money they had given him to buy stamps so that he could take their post with the rest of the collection. If residents were away for a day or two, Dave would deliver their post to a neighbour for them and the school in the village had an arrangement whereby he delivered their post to the local garage during the school holidays. In other words, Dave provided a service way beyond what he was required to do and he became a friend to all in the village. If any of the local residents passed away, Dave always attended their funerals and he and his wife, Jan, were keen attendees at the village pantomime, with Dave often the butt of some pantomime joke or other and, on one occasion, he even found himself dragged up on stage. So popular was Dave that, when he retired in 2006 after serving the parish for over 20 years, we were instrumental in arranging a surprise farewell party and presentation for him. Over 200 residents filled the village hall and a team of ladies laid on a splendid buffet, whilst a combination of John and Hazel Syms and Jan Hardman made a fantastic cake on the theme of "Postman Pat"! The very generous donations contributed by all Dave's customers resulted in him being presented with a superb flat-screen television. He and Jan were stunned and overwhelmed by the whole event and the expressions of gratitude that were forthcoming from everyone. And the villages he served were sad to lose a loyal friend.

We also became involved in another aspect of customers' post and this was helping them when they had posted letters by mistake in the box in the shop front wall. When we had first bought the shop, we inherited a key which unlocked a small door, in the inside wall of the shop, which opened the back of the letter box. Presumably, this originally meant that the owners of the shop and Post Office could empty the box and sort the post for the postman. This, however, was no longer the procedure and, as a result of re-fitting the shop, this small door was covered over. There were a number of occasions, however, when we wondered if this had been the right thing to do. We would receive telephone calls from customers who had posted letters either without addresses on the envelopes or without stamps on the letters or envelopes without their letters! They would ask, with a note of panic in their voices, whether we could rescue their letters when the postman emptied the box? We would promise to do our best and we took down relevant details to make the search easier, for instance, size or colour of the envelope involved. Our postmen were usually quite happy, with our help, to carry out this search. However, if they had already combined the contents of our letter box with the contents of an existing sack of mail, they were less than pleased and we would all end up on our knees on the shop floor, searching through an enormous heap of letters. We always found the offending envelope, however, and our absent-minded customers were delighted to retrieve their rogue mail.

One of the most enjoyable things we were able to do in the Post Office was to produce Charlton Horethorne commemorative First Day Covers for the Millennium and for the Queen's Jubilee in 2002. Special stamps had been produced for both events and for the Millennium we printed a village envelope on which we stuck the stamps. The stamps were then over-stamped with the Charlton Horethorne date stamp showing the dates of 31st December 1999 and 1st January 2000. One of each of the envelopes was presented to every child aged under 16 who lived in the parish at the time. We printed a similar envelope for the Queen's Jubilee in 2002 and stamped it up and sold the envelopes through the Post Office. They proved to be a very popular memento of a very special occasion.

Clouds in the sky

Whilst the vast majority of our life running a village shop was enjoyable, we did have a few bad times which ranged from irritations to serious occurrences. At the irritation end of the scale, when we first lived in the village the electricity supply was very susceptible to failure especially at times of high winds and storms. This is an annoyance and inconvenience on a domestic scale but it can be a nightmare when you run a shop. These power cuts always seemed to take place on wet nights between midnight and 3.00 a.m. and often triggered the alarm system, just to make matters worse. We would have to stagger out of bed, pile on warm clothes, take a torch and emerge out into a pitch black night to open up and try and establish whether it was a general power cut or just us. Given that the alarm had also been triggered we were necessarily cautious in case we had an intruder but it was always just a case of the power failure causing the fault. We then spent an hour or so covering all our chilled food in dustsheets to try and keep the temperature down and hoped that power would be restored before too long. We then had to wait for the alarm engineer to turn up to reset the security system for us. We would eventually crawl back to the cottage, wide awake, make a cup of tea and then go back to bed and try to sleep, which was usually impossible. We would just be drifting off when the alarm would go off and we would have to get up and go back next-door and see what we could salvage from the night's events. If the power had been off all night, this meant that all our chilled food would have to be thrown away and copious black bags were then taken to the tip.

Equipment breaking down was also an irritation. Freezers and chill cabinets caused us the main concern and on more than one occasion they were the cause, again, of numerous black bin bags being filled with spoiled stock and lengthy claims to the insurance company. It was also Murphy's law that they inevitably broke down just after a new consignment of stock had been delivered! Even more frustrating was when the till was not working. This could obviously happen if we had a power cut during the day but it sometimes decided to give up the ghost on its own. We then had to write down the value of everything the customer bought and add it up either in our heads or using a calculator. This is relatively straightforward when you only have one customer with a few items but when you have a queue of people waiting with baskets full of goods it can get quite stressful! Once the till was mended, we then had to key in all the day's takings to ensure that the till records were kept up to date. That was yet another job at the end of a busy and trying day. Luckily it did not happen too often but it did hone our mental arithmetic skills when it did!

One frustrating occurrence which happened outside the bounds of the shop and the cottage was the 'hole in the road'! The landscape around Charlton Horethorne is that of rolling countryside and the heart of the village is in a bowl formed by the surrounding hills. As a consequence, when it rains heavily, all the water runs off the fields and down into the centre of the village where, usually, it is transported away by the drainage system. At this point in time, however, there was a problem with the drains and the water would rush down the lanes and off the farmyard, past the shop and end up causing a flood in a house at the lowest point. The owner of this property, which had previously been the village forge, became understandably fed up with this problem and he contacted the drainage authority which eventually agreed to investigate. It appeared that the problem lay somewhere between the drain outside our cottage front garden wall and another manhole in the middle of the road outside the shop. After further investigation the conclusion was reached that the drain had probably collapsed and a hole would have to be dug to rectify the problem. The hole was duly dug between our front gate and our drive. It was approximately two metres square, and resulted in another problem being unearthed, literally! The drainage pipe which required repair was lying under a conduit carrying a mains electricity cable. Work ceased – for approximately three months! The total inability of one service supplier to communicate with another service supplier, to resolve what appeared to be a pretty straightforward issue, was staggering. The original complainant from the old forge tried every angle from letters to telephone calls to personal visits in an attempt to move the issue forward, particularly as he was still having his house flood intermittently. We joined in the fray and even involved the Parish Council at one point but the pace of action still remained unbelievably slow. Eventually the parties decided to talk to each other and the remedial work was carried out but still the hole remained. This was the responsibility of the Highways Agency, yet another body. The prevailing atmosphere around this whole project was epitomised when, one day, a bright yellow Highways truck turned up and three men got out. We were thrilled – a rather sad reflection on our state of mind but by this time 'our hole' had started to develop an eco-system of its own and was growing a fine array of weeds and wild flowers! We dashed out of the shop to welcome our saviours with open arms only to be told that "we only dig holes, we don't fill them in!" Our delight collapsed like a punctured balloon and we had to resort once again to meaningful telephone conversations with the local authority. When the hole was finally filled in we lost a village attraction which had been a talking point for nearly six months but at least the drains were working!

The least pleasant events which occurred during our time in the shop were those which involved criminality. Our first experience was not long after we became shop-keepers, when we came out of the cottage one morning to open up and found that one of the plate glass windows had a hole in it as if it had been shot with a gun. As the window was made of toughened glass the hole had not gone right through and, although the outside of the window had been crazed as a result, the inside was still alright. We called the police and when a young policewoman searched the ground outside the shop she found a shiny ball-bearing. She told us that there had been a spate of problems like this where someone was driving around and firing ball-bearings at windows and that we just seemed to be the latest victim. This appeared to us to be a particularly mindless way of passing the time and, having come to live in what we had perceived to be peaceful countryside, it was not what we had expected to happen in our first few months.

Something else which happened was equally unexpected but maybe we naively thought again that these sort of things only happened in cities. On the forecourt of the shop there was a red telephone box which, because of its age, was in fact the only listed element of the property. We did not actually own the box, it was the property of British Telecom, and, at that time, it was a box operated using cash. One night we were asleep in bed and we heard an almighty crashing and banging noise. Our bedroom overlooked the front of the property and Keith got out of bed to see what was going on. He was just in time to see someone lift the whole telephone mechanism, including the cash box, out of the telephone box and put it in the boot of a car. The car was a pretty old one and as the mechanism was heavy the car had some difficulty in pulling away but it eventually did so with a lot of revving and it disappeared up the lane. Charlton Horethorne has no street lights and there are no houses opposite the shop, just the village green, so no-one else was aware of what had happened. Keith had no chance of seeing a number plate and the occupants of the car were barely visible in the dark. We were both wide-awake by now and we debated what to do. If we called the police it could be some time before they came and as we had virtually no information to give them, the chance of them catching anyone was negligible. Also, we had to get up in a few hours time and we valued our sleep! We decided to call them in the morning. Not long after we opened the shop the following morning, a neighbouring farmer turned up in his Land Rover and handed over the phone box mechanism, minus its cash, which he had found dumped in his field. We called the police, who told us to contact BT, which we did, and they came and repaired the box and replaced the mechanism. Sadly, the phone box was attacked again in a similar way several months later but BT had found a way of making the cash mechanism much more secure and the would-be thieves just managed to wreck the box without getting away with any money. These events were unpleasant and rather un-nerving given that they were happening less than 10 metres from our bedroom window. To this day, noises outside the house at night still have us sitting up, wide awake wondering what is going on. Rather sad considering that, more often than not, it is the local wild life on a night prowl!

Much more serious were the two raids we had on the shop. Both unfortunately occurred when we were not in the shop and Catherine took the full brunt of what happened. The first raid in 1999 was an opportunistic attempt to try and steal cigarettes and alcohol. It was on a Monday afternoon, our day off, and Catherine was in the shop on her own. She had just gone into the back store to fetch something and when she returned she found a youth behind the counter helping himself to cigarettes. Despite the fact that Catherine is the village's Neighbourhood Watch co-ordinator and would, no doubt, advise anyone confronted with an intruder to back off and not 'have a go', that is precisely what she did. She rushed out and grabbed the young man and in his struggle to get free various jars of jams and pickles were swept off a circular display we had near the main door. When we arrived back from our day out at about 4.00 p.m. we were confronted by a rather shaken Catherine, a police car and a shop floor spattered with broken glass and sticky jam. We took over in the shop and Catherine and the policeman went and sat in the back office whilst we carried on the cleaning up operation. We were able to identify that several complete cartons of cigarettes had been stolen and we also had a witness who had taken the car registration number. All this had coincided with the time that the primary school children finished for the day and the lollipop lady had been very concerned at the car which had speeded past the school without stopping. As a consequence she had taken its registration number. We were horrified, however, to learn from the police that this would probably be of no use because the car was almost inevitably a 'community car'. Thoughts immediately came to mind of a vehicle provided by social services to the needy but this was far from the truth. A 'community car' in police terms is one of a group of stolen vehicles used by criminals for activities such as this and it is impossible to pin down who is using it at any one time! Having heard this depressing piece of information, we were again convinced that we were unlikely ever to see justice done as far as this event was concerned. The policeman took a vast amount of detailed information from Catherine and, by 7.00 p.m., Keith called a halt to the process as Catherine was exhausted from the events of the day and, given the unlikely success of any investigation, it seemed to be rather pointless. Keith took Catherine home and we reflected that evening on how unfortunate it had been that it had occurred whilst we had been out. We also felt a sensation which was a mixture of anger and stomach-churning sickness that honest, hard-working people such as us and our staff could be subjected to this sort of experience by people who had no intention of doing an honest day's work in their lives.

This feeling was magnified a hundred times over when we had our second serious incident in 2001. Once again we were away and once again Catherine, and on this occasion her husband, John, were our knights in shining armour. We had not had a break away from the shop for several months and so we decided to book a night at the hotel in the New Forest where we had stayed immediately after Keith retired from his job in London. This did not involve any change in staffing arrangements as we went away on Sunday afternoon and were planning to return on Monday evening, at the end of our day off. The break did not get off to an auspicious start as Sunday morning dawned grey and damp and got progressively worse with torrential rain and howling gales. We had thought that we would close the shop at 12.30 p.m., leave straight away and have a nice, cosy pub lunch en route. Instead, we had lunch at home in the hope that the weather would improve later, which it did not, so we set off at around 2.30 p.m. As it was October, it was getting dark quite early and the dreadful weather meant that, by the time we had driven through minor floods to get to our hotel, it was pitch dark and still teeming with rain. Nevertheless, we had made it and we settled down to twenty four hours of tlc! The hotel was still comfortable and well appointed but the restaurant, which had previously been superb, was having a bad night – maybe because it was a Sunday – and although our meal was generally good, all around us food was being sent back by disgruntled customers. Not quite the atmosphere we had hoped for but it was still a break and we discussed our plans for the following day.

We awoke the next morning at 6.45 a.m. to the sound of the telephone in the bedroom. Keith took the call in a state of general sleepiness which did not last very long as his face paled and the shock in his voice became evident. I had trouble working out what had happened from the one side of the conversation that I could hear and also because I was still half asleep. When Keith put the phone down his first words to me were "We've been ram-raided".

I felt sick to the stomach and all the words "why", "when", "how" came tumbling out. The phone call had been from Catherine who had been telephoned in the early hours by the landlord of our next-door pub to say that he had heard an almighty bang and then our alarm had gone off. He had got up to investigate and found that our shop front doors had been stoved in and he had immediately rushed back to the pub to call the police and Catherine. It appeared that a 4x4 vehicle had reversed at high speed into the shop doors, the occupants had jumped out, grabbed what they could and they had then sped off into the night. Catherine and John had come down to the shop to see what had happened, sort out the alarm and meet the police. It soon became evident that the doors to the shop were not going to close properly until they were repaired and this left the shop vulnerable to further attack. So, above and beyond the call of duty, Catherine and John brought sleeping bags down and slept the remainder of the night in the back store to ensure that there were no further problems. Catherine had waited until a reasonable time of the morning before calling us to tell us what had happened because she felt that there was nothing more we could do if we returned immediately. I have to confess to shedding tears at this event. They were tears of anger, tears of gratitude for what Catherine and John had done and tears at the unfairness of the action particularly when we were having the first twenty-four hour break away that we had had for months.

We dressed hurriedly and went down to a deserted restaurant and persuaded the waiter to get us some speedy breakfast although neither of us felt much like eating. We were in the car and on the road by 7.30 a.m. and back in Charlton Horethorne before 9.30 a.m. The scene that met us was shocking. The doors were badly damaged, there were tyre marks on the wood floor, stock was all over the place and evidence of the police searching for fingerprints blackened the shelves and counter. The culprits were never caught but, coincidentally, that Sunday night had been immediately prior to Pack Monday Fair in Sherborne. This is an event which goes back into the annals of history but in modern times is an annual street fair which closes the main street of Sherborne with stalls selling everything from leather goods to food. It unfortunately attracts a lot of people from outside the area, as well as from within, who are not always intent on just having a good time. The event also encompasses a travelling fairground which is set up just outside the town and which again becomes a magnet for some fairly unsavoury characters. The coincidence of our attack happening at the same time as Pack Monday Fair was not lost on the police but no direct connection could be made.

As in all things, not everything is as black as it looks. The amazing loyalty of our staff together with the overwhelming support and concern from our customers restored our faith in human nature. It was also helped by the fact that the previous day's deluge had stopped and the sun had come out! We set about getting hold of our builder to come and do a temporary job on the doors so that we could secure the shop that night. We also called our fantastic insurance agent, Richard, who came out immediately, shook his head sympathetically and gave us a claim form. We then rang our main supplier and told them what had happened and they arranged for some extra stock to be delivered to replace the cigarettes, alcohol and chocolates which had been stolen and the other goods which had been damaged. Our feet hardly touched the ground and it was only when we reflected on what had happened and what might have happened that we felt sickened. It made us very suspicious in future of any groups of unknown young men who turned up at the shop. We developed a procedure of keeping one person behind the counter and another member of staff roving in the shop where one of these young men were browsing so that they were aware that they were being observed. The door to the back store was kept closed to disguise the fact that we had a back door to the premises and any car whose occupants looked suspicious had its registration number noted. No doubt that in nine cases out of ten this was entirely unnecessary and the customers were wholly innocent but we were not going to take any chances. This attention to detail was commended by one of our customers who happened to sit on the local magistrates bench. She is a delightful lady but some of the information she happened to let slip could be unnerving, including the fact that one customer she had seen coming to our Post Office had just come out of jail having been convicted of holding up another Post Office at gunpoint! Sometimes you think that ignorance is bliss!

If this paints a depressing picture, it has to be kept in context. We only had two major problems in seven years, mercifully nobody was hurt and the damage was relatively easily rectified. Nevertheless, it was a real shock to us that we could suffer attacks such as this in a beautiful, country area and that we could have all our personal efforts and hard work violated in this way.

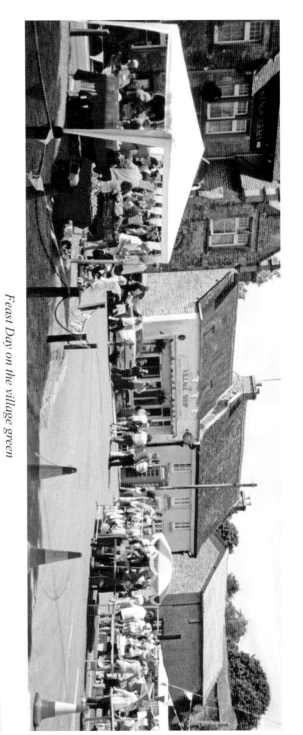

Feast Day on the village green

The Huckworthy Basset Hounds' puppy show

Celebrations in the village hall to mark the new millennium

The celebration cake made by John and Hazel Syms

*The Village Shop celebrates Queen Elizabeth II's Golden Jubilee
From l. to r. Catherine Mathew, Sue Bubb, John Mathew, Angela Goodwin, Derick Goodwin, Keith and Sue*

Angela and Derick Goodwin man the buffet in the shop

*Sue cuts the "Jubilee" cake- again made by John and Hazel Syms
– at the party in the village hall*

New Suppliers and the Challenge of being a Newsagent

For the first two and a half years that we had been open, we had worked very happily with our local wholesaler in Wincanton. In 1998, however, due to the continued increase in our business and the consequential increase in our customers' expectations, we were beginning to find the range of goods offered by our wholesaler rather limited and they were offering us no marketing support by way of promotional materials or special-offer deals. We were also noticing that the shortages on our orders each week were increasing and we were starting to become concerned that our main supplier might have some underlying problems. Around this time, we visited a major trade show – the Convenience Retail Show at the NEC in Birmingham – at which there was a wide range of exhibitors, including the symbol groups whom we had met in 1996. Over the previous two years, we had successfully built up the business and we were in possession of two years' trading figures, which gave us a more confident base from which to discuss our position. We still felt that one or two of these groups wanted to take away our independence, by either changing the fascia of the shop or imposing a range of their own products on us which would have to be ordered regularly on a monthly basis. These restrictions were not a pre-requisite from a mutual company called Londis, who offered an extremely large and comprehensive range of goods directly from their own warehouses as well as an extensive list of companies with whom they had "drop shipment" arrangements. This meant that we could order direct from the individual drop shipment companies but their invoices would go to Londis and we would pay them via the weekly Londis invoicing system in conjunction with Londis' own directly supplied goods.

We were very interested in the prospect of joining Londis, and not a little flattered, given the reaction of the symbol groups when we had approached them prior to opening! We had one or two reservations however. As mentioned previously, we did not want to lose our independent identity nor did we want to be forced into a uniform, corporate style of décor. The Londis colours were a rather vivid pea-green with orange diamonds and lettering! We expressed our concerns to the company's representative with whom we were dealing and we were assured that we could retain our current shop name and décor and we would not be forced into anything which we did not want. On that basis, we could not see how we could lose. All we had to do now was to tell our current wholesaler who had been very supportive for the previous two years. With some trepidation, we arranged to meet one of the directors of our local supplier to break the news to him. We need not have worried. Our concerns about our deliveries had apparently been well-founded as we were told that the business was closing! We thanked our lucky stars that we had met Londis at the right time and that we had taken the decision to join them.

This was the start of a very successful relationship and one that is continuing for the Village Shop to this day. The sight of the "jolly green giant", as the enormous pea-green Londis lorry became known, is now a regular one in the village and the delivery driver, Andy, was almost one of our team by the time we left. He and Keith were both ardent football fans, albeit for different teams, and once the delivery was stacked in the back store there was always a good quarter of an hour spent discussing the previous weekend's football results! Apart from the much wider range of goods and suppliers which Londis offered, they also had a number of in-house services into which we could tap if we so wished. These ranged from over-the-phone advice on particular products to complete marketing reviews of the business including product mix and shop layout. They also gave us significant marketing support with promotional material and monthly special offers.

Ordering products from Londis was done on a weekly basis and it was done electronically. Once we got used to the system we found it very easy to use and, in general, we had very few problems with it. The basis of the system was an enormous catalogue of products, which was issued three-weekly, and against each product there was a barcode. We had an electronic 'gun' with which we swiped the code and entered the number of units we required. Once we had completed the order, the system was plugged into the telephone line and the order was transmitted down the telephone line. Nine times out of ten this worked brilliantly but there was the odd occasion when the order just would not transmit. Panic than set in. Usually it was only a temporary problem with the computer at the depot but there was one occasion when we had to hand-write the whole order, with all the product codes, quantities etc., and fax it to the warehouse. This took ages! Obviously, there was also an enormous capacity at our end for human error, particularly in the early days! We soon perfected the method of deleting an order from the system when we found that we had either swiped the wrong product or placed an order for a number of units far in excess of what we needed. The proof of the pudding was always in the eating when the lorry came on a Tuesday and suddenly you spied a product in one of the delivery cages that you knew you did not stock! Was it our confused ordering or had the wrong product been picked in the warehouse? I have to say that, although it did not happen too often, it was more likely to be the latter than the former. It was not unusual to find, a computer generated label printed, say, for a carton of toilet rolls stuck on a carton of dog food! Product identification was obviously not high on the skills inventory in the Londis warehouse!

In 1998, we were made aware that, as part of the overall support for village shops, South Somerset District Council were making available limited grants for the purchase of capital equipment, as opposed to stock, to enable village shops to improve their businesses. The basis of the grant was an award of up to £5000 with the shop owners matching the award from their own funds. Due to our expanding business, we identified the need for an additional chill unit, extra shelving and a new computer which would support our "back office" operations. A substantial amount of research was inevitably required as we had to obtain three separate quotations from, what turned out to be, three companies in each category. It was all worth it, however, because we obviously made a good business case as we received a grant of £3015 towards our purchases.

Having decided to increase our shelf space due to our ever-burgeoning number of products, we thought that this would be a good time to invest in some expert help from Londis. We ordered our extra shelving from our original shop-fitter and another chill unit from a local supplier. Once they were installed, we had a team from Londis visit the shop and, over two days, re-layout the stock to take advantage of the extra display area. This exercise was of mixed success. The successful aspect was that customers seemed to see the stock with new eyes and exclaimed with delight that we now stocked a product which we had, in fact, had on the shelves from the beginning! The less successful part of the exercise was the team of young men who were left with us to carry out the shelf-stacking of the new layout. They had been given detailed layout diagrams to work from but their work rate was not what you would call fast and it was not helped by the fact that we had the pub next door. Each lunch time they disappeared into the pub for their "lunch" and when they came out they proceeded to play football in the road outside the shop making it difficult for our customers to come and go without being bowled over or hit on the head! We were not best pleased and expressed our displeasure to the team themselves and their bosses at head office. Ultimately, however, the job was completed and, overall, it was a success even if it only meant that we felt we had not been doing such a bad job ourselves without having a degree in marketing!

One of the omissions in our ever-increasing range of products had been fresh meat. From the very start we had decided that the legislation and health hazards associated with running anything approaching a delicatessen were too much of a burden and we had only stocked pre-packed cold meat, cheese, sausages etc. In 2000, a young man turned up one day and invited us to go and look at the range of pre-packed fresh meat which he had in his van and which he said he was already supplying to a number of outlets in the area. The range was impressive and we were particularly interested because all of the meat was local and a high proportion of it was organic. The young man who had called on us turned out to be a member of a farming family who farmed approximately ten miles away and had expanded their farm shop into the pre-packed market for local shops. Given the short shelf-life of these sorts of items, we were also very interested to learn that they were prepared to operate on a sale or return basis and that they would stock our chill for us and come two or three times a week to replace out of date stock with fresh produce. This seemed to be a win-win situation.

Our customers were delighted to be able to buy fresh local meat and soon the stock was becoming very popular, particularly the home-made sausages in a variety of flavours. We did have some problems with this new venture, however, including what appeared to be a lack of communication between the member of the farming family who did the deliveries and took any orders and the other members of the family who put the orders together! Another problem was fresh meat and hot weather! Because of the plate-glass windows and the various chill and freezer units churning out hot air, the shop tended to get very hot in the summer and this was not always good news for our meat. We would check the dates on, for instance, fresh chickens to make sure that they were well in date but occasionally we would detect a rather unpleasant whiff emanating from our poultry! These then had to be stored in a fridge in the back store until the next collection from the butcher and, I have to say that, sometimes, the air in the fridge was not too pleasant! We eventually came to an agreement with the farm that they would reduce the shelf-life dates on our chickens in the summer and not deliver so many to us. This seemed to solve the problem and everyone was happy!

One of our other new suppliers in the last couple of years that we were in the shop was Salcombe Dairy. The name is relatively self-explanatory in that they were based in Salcombe in Devon but they made the most delicious ice-cream and sorbet in a wide range of flavours. We were first put on to them by my parents who had come across their ice-cream when staying in a hotel in Devon and they had made the journey over to

Salcombe to buy some ice-cream direct to bring home with them. So addicted to it did they become that they asked us if we could stock it and this was the start of a whole new range of products which the shop still stocks today. Along with all the usual flavours we had such delights as blackcurrant, rum and raisin and honeycomb as well as an amazing Christmas pudding flavoured ice-cream for Christmas. It was not a cheap option for a dessert but it certainly knocked soft-scoop vanilla into a cocked hat!

During our seven-year ownership of the shop we also had an enforced change of newspaper wholesaler. As I mentioned earlier, we inherited WH Smith as our supplier of newspapers and magazines and the cartel that operates in this field meant that we had no option but to use them. Similarly, we had no say in the matter when WH Smith sold their business to a company called Surridge Dawson. The impact on us was not significant as they still operated from Yeovil, about 10 miles away, and we still received our deliveries with an earth-shattering thump at about 6.00 a.m. in the morning. Newspapers and magazines are the original "sale or return" item with unsold daily newspapers being bundled up each night for collection, by a separate van, at an even more unearthly time in the early hours of the morning. Magazines are also on sale or return but this system was more complicated. Magazines could be weekly, monthly, quarterly or any combination of the three and we were only allowed to return them at designated times. If we missed the allotted period we ended up being billed for unsold editions. Whilst I was predominantly in charge of the Post Office, Keith took on the unenviable task of managing the supply and return of newspapers and magazines.

The first problem was stopping the wholesaler bombarding us with unwanted titles. They seemed very keen to deluge us with quiz magazines and children's comics, both of which we wanted to stock but not in the variety and quantity they envisaged. Keith would spend hours on the telephone to Surridge Dawson amending our standing order list, which had magically grown to include innumerable unwanted titles. Another nightmare was the endless variety of "part-works" with which we were issued and which, if we did not return them at the right time, were a very expensive, virtually un-saleable product. It did not take very long to establish that there were very few people in the village who wanted to pay anything from £5 to £8 per copy for a magazine which would, eventually, after up to 100 editions, provide you with all the pieces to make, for instance, the "Mary Rose"! If there was such an unfortunate individual, you could bet your bottom dollar that the wholesaler would forget to send us one copy and Keith then spent an inordinate amount of time trying to get a "back- copy", which could take weeks to achieve. Alternatively, the right copies were delivered but the special "collectable" attached to the front of the magazine was damaged – we were into the back-copy nightmare again. We did in fact have one customer who was collecting all these magazines to make a different historical ship model. He came in one day in total despair because, to be helpful, his daughter had opened all the packets containing the various components and tipped them into a pile for her father to make up. He had absolutely no idea which piece was which or what to do with them! On this occasion we were unable to help!

The other component of the newspaper business was the infamous "newspaper voucher" system. Several of the national newspapers, lead predominantly by The Daily Telegraph, introduced a voucher system which allowed their regular customers to pay up-front for up to a year's newspapers and thereby purchase their papers at a discount. As a newspaper retailer, we were sent books of vouchers allocated to specific customers which we had to tear out and return to the wholesaler in the relevant week. For carrying out this service we received full payment for the newspaper sold plus the princely sum of 1p per paper for our trouble. As we had to either send the vouchers recorded delivery in the post, to ensure that we had confirmation of their safe arrival, or we had to drive to Yeovil and deliver the vouchers in person, 1p per copy was not excessive payment! Tearing out the vouchers from their various books and integrating them with the individual vouchers we had received from customers during the week was a Sunday morning job. They then had to be grouped in their individual categories, 1p off The Mail, free News of the World, pre-paid Daily Telegraph etc. etc. etc., and entered on the pre-printed form issued by the wholesaler – which never seemed to have the variety of vouchers we had received! We also never quite got over the customers, predominantly Daily Telegraph readers whose vouchers were sent to us in a book, who would come in and ask for a couple of days' vouchers out of their book because they were going away for the weekend and wanted a free paper at their chosen destination.

The other aspect of newspapers which always caused problems was the various supplements which the weekend newspapers contained. When we started in the shop we were not aware that all these supplements came separately from the main newspaper and therefore, as newsagents, we had to "stuff" the supplements into their appropriate papers. This added enormously to our workload on a Saturday and Sunday morning and we had papers and supplements strewn all over the counter, the newspaper table and the top of the chest freezer whilst we married all the various pieces together. Luckily we had taken the decision from the start not to operate newspaper rounds but, in the first year or so, Pam and Colin, our Sunday morning deliverers, had increasing difficulty in delivering these hefty wadges to customers' houses. They either had to be taken apart and fed through letter boxes in their individual parts or some customers got wise to the possibility of their large papers being torn during this process and left carrier bags hanging on their doors into which the complete papers could be placed. Inevitably we received comments every weekend about the inordinate waste of paper that these publications contained but these comments were balanced by the complaints we received if a particular supplement was missing. It was an unwritten rule that if a supplement was missing it was bound to be the only one that that particular customer wanted! Having spent some considerable time compiling the papers in the morning, insult was added to injury if we had had a quiet weekend for newspaper sales and we then had to bundle together mammoth piles of needlessly compiled newspapers for returning to the wholesaler!

Innovations and Replacements

During the course of our seven year ownership of the shop, we invested in a number of new pieces of kit for the shop, either because of necessity or because we thought they would improve the overall operation of the business. Our first investment was a machine which was affectionately called the "zapper". In the early days of our business we were plagued in the summer with flies, and in the early autumn, with wasps. The former were just a nuisance but the latter could send customers scurrying for the door which was not too good for business. The "zapper" was an electrical device which attracted flying beasts and, rather unpleasantly, sizzled them on the exposed elements. The more squeamish of our customers did not appreciate the noise as a large wasp met its frying end but small boys seemed to find the whole process a real attraction!

Charlton Horethorne is one of many villages in the country which shuns the installation of street lights meaning that, in the winter, the village is pitched into complete darkness from about 5.00 p.m. onwards. There are disadvantages, such as going to a friend's house in the daylight and emerging several hours later, without a torch, and having to find your way home by trying to visualise almost invisible landmarks. Having said this, the advantages far outweigh the disadvantages particularly the panorama of stars and planets clearly visible above your head like an enchanting ballroom ceiling. The lights from the houses in the village provide beacons of light at ground level and we soon realised that, although we had plate glass windows in the shop and bright, modern internal lighting, the shop did not stand out prominently from the road when it was dark. Extra lighting was called for and we invested in a set of rather smart brass lights which brought the front of the shop from, in the stellar analogy, a glowing, distant planet to a bright, shining star. It was always comforting when we had been out on one of our winter days off to come down the hill into the village and see our home and business beaming out a welcome to us.

The cost of electricity used in the shop was always a concern predominantly because of the chill and freezer units. Unexpectedly, this was particularly high in the summer because the chill units and freezers had to work harder to keep cool in the hot shop and in working harder they produced more warm air which made the shop even hotter – and so on and so on! One investment which we made which proved to be a false one was on a device called Sava-Watt. This purported to reduce one's electricity consumption by more efficiently using the electricity in the equipment to which it was connected. We did all the research we could, including talking to our electricity supplier and to consumer organisations. Whilst the response we received did not categorically confirm the success of this device, the indications were that it would improve the efficiency of our consumption so we went ahead and leased the equipment and had it fitted to our chill units. It turned out to be a waste of money! There was no appreciable difference in our electricity bills and we ended up paying the leasing costs for a number of years. You live and learn!

Some innovations were forced on us, for instance the introduction of metric scales in 2000. There was a lot of national resistance to the change from Imperial to metric weights and various shopkeepers and stall-holders appeared on national television swearing to continue weighing their bananas using Imperial weights to the day they died. Of course this did not happen and we were all informed that change-over day was due and that we had to sell goods by kilograms not by pounds. This necessitated us buying completely new scales which was a bit frustrating because our existing ones were perfectly good. However, we found that the cost of converting them was far in excess of buying new ones so we bit the bullet and invested in our brand spanking new metric scales. It took us a bit of time to get used to pricing our loose goods, such as fruit and vegetables, in kilograms – we were all of an age where pounds and ounces ruled! Some of our elderly customers had a lot of difficulty adjusting, so we were constantly doing mental conversions for them because they were convinced that, with the change in weighing method, all the prices had gone up as well. What we had not expected was a spot check out of the blue from a man from Trading Standards who came to check our new scales to ensure that they conformed to the new regulations. Luckily they did – there were quite hefty fines for anyone found selling goods either under the old Imperial system or via scales which were shown to be defective. Ironically, in 2007 the EU ruled that retailers could display both metric and Imperial weights and measures, so one has to wonder whether all the cost and heartache were worthwhile.

Our other major improvement was more by way of a reinstatement of something which had first been done when we opened, i.e. our polished wood floor. Despite regular sweeping and washing, the floor in the shop, which had been beautifully golden and shiny in July 1996, was now, in 2002, looking decidedly dull and in need of further attention. At that time, the Village Hall Committee was chaired by a gentleman called John Syms and he was ably assisted by another retired villager, Alf Titheridge. Both these men had had connections with the building trade and they had personally carried out a lot of improvements to the fabric of the Village Hall since they had been on the Committee. One of the improvements they had been responsible for was the restoration of the sprung, wood floor in the Hall, including polishing and re-sealing it. One day, John came into the shop and commented on the deterioration of our wood floor. He said that he and Alf had some varnish left from doing the Hall floor and they would happily come up one weekend and do the shop floor for us. We jumped at the offer. So, one sunny Sunday, when we closed at lunch time, we removed everything possible from the floor and John and Alf set about refurbishing it for us. It was a long, hot job and the smell of the varnish was almost over-powering in the shop but they completed it and the result was magnificent. They ended the day sitting in our garden with cans of cold lager and we, once again, had a shop floor to be proud of. That is what you call the best of village life!

VILLAGE EVENTS

Life in a village takes on all sorts of hues and is very like the life in a large family. There are happy events, sad events, good times, bad times and whilst the members of the village "family" can, and do, fall out with each other they certainly pull together when it matters. Pulling together to raise funds for village activities and heritage is one example, although the subject of the fund raising can also sometimes be one for debate. This was true when, in 2002, an appeal was launched to have the church bells taken down to be restored, re-tuned and to have them re-hung in the bell tower in an improved frame. The cost of this was going to run to a sizeable five-figure amount and there was some concern in the village about the expense involved Despite these village rumblings, the project gained momentum and a working group was formed to raise the money. The gentleman who chaired this group was a retired high-ranking diplomat whose last posting before retirement had been in the British Embassy in Shanghai. He was heard to say, when the project finally reached a successful conclusion, that he had found it far easier to deal with the Chinese than with all the bodies, officials and individuals involved in restoring a set of English village church bells!

The money for the restoration was raised, predominantly, at a few very successful and well-attended village events where the attendees were extremely generous with their cheque books. However, the most original fund-raiser, which was organised by Catherine Mathew, was Cowpat Roulette! We were at a loss to understand how this would work until she gave us a run down of the event. At the time, her father's farm was home to a dairy herd being farmed by another local farmer and they resided in a field beside Catherine's father's farmhouse. Catherine drew a boxed grid on an A3 sheet of paper with letters across the top and numbers down the side and then staked out the designated field to match the grid. We had the A3 sheet displayed in the shop and customers were invited to buy a square at £1 each based on where they thought the first cow would drop the first cowpat! On a warm Saturday afternoon, a crowd of villagers gathered around the edge of the designated field and two cows were herded in. It was a bizarre sight to see the intense way that grown men and women were studying cows' rear ends and trying to encourage likely looking animals into their own preferred area of the field. Suddenly the cry went up and a startled looking cow was cheered as she performed on a particular contestant's patch of grass! It was a fun afternoon that you would only encounter in the country and it raised a lot of money for the bells appeal!

Once sufficient funds were raised, the date could be set for the bells to be removed from the tower to start their long journey to the foundry in Whitechapel in London where they were going to be restored. Once they had arrived in London, the bell-ringers and a number of other villagers travelled to the foundry to be shown around and to have explained to them exactly what the restoration involved. The party arrived back in the village with fascinating tales of what they had seen, not least the description of the foundry which had been in existence for several hundred years and which, by all accounts, had hardly changed in that time!

The eight bells, with ages ranging from the 14th century to the 19th century, were finally removed from the tower, with some difficulty as they collectively weighed several tons. A traditional 'Bell-Pull Carnival' took place when the bells were removed from the tower and just before they were taken to the bell foundry. Seven bells were lined up on the church path, ready to be loaded onto the lorry. The treble bell was lifted onto a decorated trailer and pulled around the village by an old Ferguson tractor, followed by various other decorated floats. At the end of the procession, the bell was loaded onto the lorry with the other six and taken up to Whitechapel. Before they set off, the lorry driver lifted the treble bell high up on his crane and made it swing up in the air before lowering it down onto the lorry!

Whilst the bells were in London, the work on the new steel bell frame was completed, not without the odd hitch, and the village awaited the return of the restored bells with great anticipation. Once they were re-hung, the bells were re-dedicated by Bishop Peter of Bath and Wells at a very special Harvest Festival service. The whole process had been a very special event which will probably not be seen again for 120 years, the length of time since the previous restoration.

One of the highlights of annual village life is the village bonfire party and fireworks display which always takes place on 5th November and which is organised by the tireless Catherine and her husband, John. It takes a great deal of organisation to lay on a public display like this and, also, a considerable amount of money, which Catherine sets about raising each year. Her methods of fund raising have been many and various. One year, she sent each house in the village a tube of Smarties and asked the occupants to fill it with coins by a certain date and return it to her – after eating the Smarties! This was quite a smart move – no pun intended – as only 1p, 5p, 20p and £1 coins would fit in the tubes, and whilst the children could put their 5p's and 1p's aside, most adults felt obliged to donate 20p's and £1's so it was rather a profitable exercise. Another method of fund raising was to hold regular car boot sales on the pub car park and these proved to be popular pulling in sellers and buyers from outside the village.

The annual bonfire party and fireworks display had gained an excellent reputation not only in the village but in surrounding areas and the audience was always large and appreciative. In our early days in the village, the party was held on a field just off the centre of the village. However, this field was partially transformed into the commemorative Millennium Green in 2000 and the landscaped part of the Green made an excellent area from which the crowds could watch the display taking place in the remaining part of the field. It was in this latter area that the bonfire was built. Catherine and a team of helpers would collect up any combustible material from the village in the weeks leading up to the display and then, on the Saturday morning before the event, there would be a general invitation to help build the bonfire. The organisation behind the whole display was significant and required Catherine and her team of "firework lighters" to attend courses and gain approval before they were licensed to hold the event. Red Cross volunteers were always in attendance but luckily, to date, have never been needed but, in fact, they seemed to be glad to come along just to enjoy the occasion. Teams of volunteers were lined up to make and serve mulled wine as well as soft drinks for the children and other helpers in the village transported and heated vast quantities of home made soup for those who wanted an alternative type of warming. Stephen and Joyce Hall, a retired accountant and his wife, nobly transported their barbecue down to the Green and spent 2 or 3 hours being gradually kippered whilst they produced endless hotdogs and beef-burgers. There were always concerns about sparks flying from the bonfire, particularly as there were several thatched properties in the vicinity. To ensure that there were no problems later in the night, after the party was over, Catherine and John would get up in the early hours of the morning to make sure that the bonfire had not flared up and it was not causing any problems. The following morning they then walked the neighbouring fields to collect any rocket sticks which had fallen from the sky and which could potentially be a problem to livestock. It was, and still is, one of the most popular events in the village and it is all down to one or two people dedicated to preserving the tradition.

The other tradition in the village which, sadly, has lapsed for the time being, is that of Feast Day. The origins of Feast Day are both ancient and slightly unclear. One account has it that it is connected with a church festival, possibly that of the village church's Patron Saint, St. Peter, on 29th June. However, in 1293 a Charter was procured from Edward I for a weekly Market to be held in the village and a Fair yearly on the eve and day of St. Thomas the Martyr. Whatever the origins, Feast Day in our time in the village has ranged from the traditional summer fete with stalls, majorettes, hoopla and coconut shies, to a display of vintage tractors, an armoured vehicle loaned by the Army, a boules competition in the pub car park, a gymnastics display by the local school children and a dog show. It was always a busy day in the shop for us as we were open all day on the Saturday of the event. As with all things, there is usually a small and dedicated team of villagers who, year after year, organise such events and you can only flog a horse so long. Regrettably no-one came forward to carry on the organisation and so, in 2005, Feast Day ceased to happen. Hopefully it will be resurrected at some time but in the 21st century, with so many other leisure-time distractions, it is very difficult to lay on an event which attracts enough people to not only make it viable but also to raise funds for other village organisations.

As I mentioned earlier, at the time that we came to the village there were two hunt kennels in the village and hunting was very much part of village life. When, towards the end of our time in the shop, there were political moves to ban hunting with dogs, we maintained a very neutral stance. Whatever our personal feelings were towards hunting, we were in business and our customers had a range of opinions which we felt we had to respect. We did, however, see the ugly side of the opposition to hunting. One weekend, the basset hounds were due to hunt and they met in the pub car park, opposite the shop, before setting off. Within minutes of them congregating, a number of cars drew up and a group of individuals got out wearing combat dress, balaclava helmets and gloves and carrying walkie-talkie radios. It was obvious that they were intent on stopping the hunt and they were certainly very menacing. They had not, however, counted on the owner of the hunt and her staff and she was having no truck with such interference. She defied their intimidation and the hunt set off as planned. Luckily there did not appear to be any violent intent but it was not a very pleasant experience.

Another, apparently menacing occurrence, eventually had a funny side to it. The village, just before we had arrived, had experienced a number of burglaries and the residents were very jittery, particularly of vehicles which appeared to be cruising the village for no good reason. It is difficult not be affected by such nervousness so when, one morning, we came out to unlock the shop and saw a car parked on the opposite side of the road with two rather scruffy men in it, we were concerned. We went into the shop and, unusually for us, locked the door behind us. As we put the newspapers together and stacked the milk we kept looking out of the window and eventually the car pulled away. We sighed a sigh of relief which was only short lived when the car reappeared and parked in the pub car park. By this stage we were getting very concerned as we were due to open and thoughts of gun-toting villains were becoming uppermost in our thoughts. We decided to telephone Catherine who, as the village's neighbourhood watch co-ordinator, was always the first to be informed by the police of any problems likely from the criminal fraternity. Our telephone call was reassuring and rather ironic. It turned out that our two "suspicious characters" were actually undercover policemen who were not best pleased that the local police station had been inundated with telephone calls from Charlton Horethorne residents reporting the sighting of possible villains. Their cover, involving the surveillance of a local resident for alleged smuggling activities, was well and truly blown! Such is the vigilance of country folk.

A little more vigilance by the pub landlord might have been a good idea when, on one occasion, the pub caught fire! As was our wont, given our early start, we had gone to bed at around 9.30 p.m. and were happily in the land of nod when we were awoken by the flashing of blue lights coming through our bedroom curtain. Keith jumped out of bed and, looking out of the window, came virtually face to face with a fire engine. We had no idea at that stage where the fire was but, visualising our business going up in flames, we threw on some clothes in our groggy, dopey state and went outside. We were greeted by the landlord coughing and spluttering outside the pub, his elderly father in law and their dog standing in the road looking bemused and the customers who had been inside at the time of the evacuation staring at the smoking building with their pint glasses grasped firmly in their hands. It transpired that a deep fat fryer in the kitchen had caught fire and caused a tremendous amount of smoke which had necessitated evacuating the building and calling the fire brigade. It did not take too long to put out the fire and the damage was predominantly due to the smoke and water. To show his appreciation for their efforts, the landlord went back into the pub and pulled pints for all the fire crew who then leant on the fire engine and downed their beer. We could only hope that they were not called to another fire that night! During the course of all this drama, the landlord's wife returned from a dinner she had been attending and there were the inevitable comments about not being able to leave him in charge of anything for very long! Whilst all this had been going on, we had taken the landlord's father in law and their dog into the house so that he could sit down somewhere away from the smoke and general mayhem. We eventually persuaded him to stay the night with us and I made up the bed in the spare room and he was able to enjoy some peace and quiet. I think we finally got to bed at about 12.30 a.m. Who says life in the country is boring?

Outstanding Occasions
– of one sort and another

I think the first outstanding event we enjoyed whilst we owned the shop was the first anniversary of our re-opening it. We had had a very successful and enjoyable first year and we wanted to celebrate it with our customers and thank them for welcoming us to the village. We decided to arrange a first anniversary party in the shop one July Saturday morning in 1997. We laid on some finger buffet food and some wine and our master of ceremonies was once again John Mathew. We borrowed some tables from the village hall and had them out on the shop forecourt where people could sit and chat, eat and drink and generally enjoy what turned out to be a beautiful sunny day. It was a thoroughly pleasant occasion and one which marked the end of a year of hard work which had paid off in every way possible.

The approach of the end of the 20th century heralded all sorts of plans in the village for celebrations to mark the end of the millennium. It was also felt that a lasting testament to the end of the 1900's should be included in the plans and this was the catalyst for the development of a new village green. The Millennium Green, as it is now known, was a field behind a group of five or six houses in the centre of the village and it was the site of the annual village bonfire party which I mentioned earlier. Approximately half to two thirds of the field was earmarked for the new Green and it included such things as a pond, a bog area, mown grass areas, new trees, a stone shelter and seat and a small playground for younger children with swings and a slide. There was also a raised terraced area overlooking the pond, the stone wall of which was made up of numbered stones. Incorporated in the stone wall was a list of all the children in the village primary school at the turn of the century and each child was allocated a numbered stone. Buried within the construction was a time capsule containing various pieces of information and memorabilia about the village in the year 1999 and in a grassed area next to the playground the school children planted daffodil bulbs in the pattern of "2000".

The production of something lasting to commemorate the start of a new millennium got us thinking, albeit on a very much smaller scale, and the idea we came up with ended up having a much larger impact than we could possibly have imagined. Our idea concerned the red BT telephone box outside the shop. When we bought the shop, we were made aware by our solicitor of the fact that we had a telephone box, which we did not own, on our forecourt outside the shop and that this box was in fact a 'listed' property. This was the only area of our property which was 'listed' and as such should have been well looked after as an example of an historic piece of telephonic equipment. But it was not! The paint was peeling, the windows were in fact pieces of Perspex, which were discoloured and crazed by age, and all in all the phone box was a disgrace. During 1999, I decided that our contribution to a lasting improvement to the fabric of the village would be to get the phone box restored to its former glory, so I wrote to BT.

Not a lot happened for quite a while and then we heard from BT that they had agreed to carry out the restoration of our phone box and we were thrilled that we had in fact achieved something for the village. In due course, true to their word, a van arrived and a man started work on the box. He removed all the crazed Perspex windows, he rubbed down the paintwork and painted the phone box in grey undercoat and he left. The weeks went by and nothing happened. Far from being impressed by our initiative, the villagers who used the phone box were less than impressed that the windows had been removed and that the wind and rain blew relentlessly through the open holes whilst they made their phone calls. 1999 was coming to an end and still nothing happened and all our pestering of BT seemed to be getting nowhere. In the end we wrote a meaningful letter to the department dealing with the restoration hoping that this would at least stir them into action. The response we received was verging on the farcical. BT denied having even started the work and said that they had no record of a restoration project in Charlton Horethorne! We were flabbergasted and immediately got on the phone to the sender of the letter. This telephone call did nothing to restore our faith in BT. The lady at the other end of the phone reiterated the fact that BT had never even started work on the phone box and when we pointed out that the windows had all been removed she said the box must have been vandalised! She did however concede that this was unlikely when we pointed out that the vandals had also painted the box in grey undercoat!

By now we were in the year 2000 and our attempt to get the phone box restored for the millennium was behind schedule to say the least. In March 2000 we went away for two weeks' holiday in the Caribbean (our eventual honeymoon) and we left Catherine and Sue in charge of the shop and Post Office. We should have anticipated a problem had it registered with us that we were going to be away for 1st April! The first we knew of some unauthorised events going on in the shop was when a fax was slid under the door of our hotel room. The fax read something like "urgent problem with telephone box, come home immediately"! When we realised the date of the fax, we soon cottoned on and we faxed back "decided to expand chain of shops to Caribbean, not coming home, over to you"! This, however, was only half the story as we found out when we got home. Having staff with a sense of humour is a real bonus but this time they had surpassed themselves! Unbeknown to us, in our absence, Catherine and Sue had drawn up a "save our phone box" petition and they started telling people that the phone box was going to be removed, hence BT's failure to finish the restoration. This, of course, was a load of nonsense but so credible were they that they soon had pages of signatures on the petition. One of our customers was so enraged that he stormed home and immediately got on the phone to the Chairman of BT and berated him for removing such a valued village amenity! Eventually, the perpetrators of the April Fool came clean and the village was impressed if a little shame-faced that they had been so comprehensively taken-in!

Eventually, in the late spring of 2000, we persuaded BT to send out a surveyor and, when he reviewed the evidence, he reluctantly agreed that work had in fact been started on the phone box. It appeared that BT sub-contracted the maintenance work to a third party and BT had changed contractors just after the initial stripping out of the box. The new contractor had not been passed details of the job and therefore denied any knowledge of an incomplete restoration. The story had a happy ending in that, by the summer of 2000, we had a gleaming red, newly glazed telephone box but I must admit that there were times when I wondered why I had ever started the whole exercise.

The celebrations for Millennium Day itself began with a service in the village church and then afterwards there was a party in the village hall with a buffet lunch, to which just about all the village came. Hazel and John Syms made a magnificent Millennium cake and there was a marquee attached to the hall in which there were bales of hay over, on and around which the children of the village played. Prior to the Day, a village photograph was arranged on the Millennium Green and the elderly gentleman who took the photograph balanced precariously on top of a ladder whilst several hundred people jostled to ensure that they could be seen. Also, to commemorate the occasion, a beautiful plate was produced illustrated with scenes of the village and information about the village detailed in gold on the back. All in all, Charlton Horethorne did its very best to ensure that we marked the turn of the century in a memorable fashion.

The next momentous occasion came in 2002 when the nation and Charlton Horethorne in particular celebrated Queen Elizabeth II's Golden Jubilee. All the events took place between Thursday 30th May and Monday 3rd June which was declared a national Bank Holiday. On the Thursday the primary school children in the village school held a children's disco and this was followed on the Friday with a "street party" in the school playground, where each of the children was presented with a Jubilee commemorative coin. In the evening, there was the first of two performances of a variety show held in the village hall with local residents providing entertainment spanning the Queen's fifty year reign. For us in the shop, our main contribution to these celebrations was on the Saturday morning when we held a Jubilee Celebration Party. We had decked out the shop in red, white and blue and Union Jack bunting and we laid on a buffet which was manned very ably by friends of ours in the village, Derick and Angela Goodwin. Although we usually employed the services of John Mathew to dispense wine and other drinks, on this occasion we engaged his other major talent and that was as musician. John set up his keyboard on the forecourt outside the shop and serenaded the crowds which were gathered inside and out. Once again we were blessed with the weather – it was a beautiful, cloudless, sunny day. We and our staff were all decked out in red, white and blue with glittery hats and, much to everyone's amusement, I wore red, white and blue striped tights! In retrospect I did look rather like a patriotic bee! We had also organised a children's fancy dress competition with the theme of 'royalty' and there were a good crowd of fantastically dressed children lined up on the village green outside the shop for judging by local senior resident, Adela Dyson. The ultimate winners were Charlotte and Alexander Radford, who both wore magnificent regal costumes, but all the others, and their mothers, had put a tremendous amount of effort into the competition and everyone received a prize! Our party started around 11.00 a.m. and we finally wound everything up in the early afternoon having had a marvellous morning and one which we certainly will never forget.

The second performance of the variety show took place on the Saturday evening and, as another mark of the great occasion, a quarter peal of bells was rung on the village church bells. More events were scheduled for the Bank Holiday Monday but sadly the weather was not so kind to us. There was to be a Service of Thanksgiving on the new Millennium Green followed by the official opening of the children's play area on the Green, a village photograph and then a village picnic with games and a tug of war. The day dawned grey, damp and breezy and it threatened to ruin all the plans for the early part of the day. However, in true British fashion, we were not that easily put off and a large number of people braved the elements and gathered on the Green for the Service. Due to the weather, a temporary gazebo had been erected in which Bill Closs, the provider of the musical accompaniment, could safely play his keyboard without fear of electrocution.

The vicar, Peter Hallett, arrived wearing his clerical, black cloak over his cassock and one of our neighbours commented that he looked like the Grim Reaper! We stoutly continued through the Service, sheltering under umbrellas and trying to keep warm by singing extra loudly! We had planned, with half a dozen other friends, to club together and picnic on the Green after the Service. However, given the inclement conditions, everyone came to our house with their picnics, we spread the rugs on the lounge floor and had a very enjoyable and rather alcoholic 'indoor picnic' whilst watching the celebrations going on in London on the television. Some of the younger and more hardy members of the village did manage to have their picnic on the Green, as the rain eventually stopped, and they then competed in a number of crazy outdoor games to keep themselves warm. Later in the afternoon, the whole village congregated in the village hall where an exhibition of memorabilia, loaned by local residents, was on display illustrating life at the time of the Queen's Coronation. A beautiful Jubilee cake, once again provided and decorated by Hazel and John Syms, was cut and the Queen's health was toasted with a glass of 'bubbly'. All the children in the parish were presented with a Jubilee mug. The last event of the day was not actually in the village but was on Corton Denham Hill, just outside Charlton Horethorne. At a designated time in the evening, beacons were lit throughout the country to provide national lines of light and Corton Denham Hill was one of the sites chosen. This was a fitting end to a celebration in which the whole nation had participated and Charlton Horethorne had certainly contributed in a fitting and enthusiastic manner.

The other national events, which occurred in 1997 and 2001, were two general elections. We decided from the outset that we would not display any particular political party's posters or other literature in the shop as we felt that we were more than likely to have customers of every political persuasion and we did not wish to cause offence to anyone. We also wanted to keep our own political opinions to ourselves as we did not want to be drawn into any political debates or be seen to be supporting one party over another. We kept to this policy throughout our shop-owning days but there were occasions when we had to step in to stop the shop being used for political propaganda. Historically, the village and surrounding areas had been a Conservative party stronghold and Conservative allegiances were still very strong despite the party faltering nationally. Having taken our non-party-political stance, we were somewhat taken aback by the first piece of overt canvassing which took place involving the shop. Early one afternoon in 1997, I was in the shop on my own when I saw a number of local residents starting to congregate on the shop forecourt. I was puzzled because I could think of no reason for them to be gathering, there was no bus due, it was not the day for the mobile library and as far as I knew none of the village groups had an outing planned. It was also puzzling because a number of the people standing outside the shop were not exactly regular shoppers, more the people who simply came in for their newspapers. The next thing that happened was that a car pulled up, sporting Conservative banners, and several people got out including a gentleman wearing a large blue rosette. One of the party then started to line up the assembled throng outside the shop and take photographs. I was infuriated. No-one had had the courtesy of coming into the shop and asking if we minded being used in this way, either before what was obviously a planned event or during it. I stormed out and asked who was in charge of this exercise and a bemused Conservative candidate and, presumably, his agent came into the shop to apologise. To be fair to them they had asked a local party member to check with us whether we minded and they had been given the impression that we were happy to go along with the arrangement. Matters did not end there, however, because later that day we learnt that the photographs which had been taken were destined to be included in some party literature bemoaning the Labour government's treatment of village shops. It took a number of telephone calls to the local Conservative constituency office to obtain assurances that the photograph of our shop would not be used in their literature. I think what upset us most was that there was an underlying arrogance about the way the matter had been handled coupled with a complete lack of common courtesy. Unfortunately, lessons were not learned and we had a similar experience at the next General Election with the same political party. The only saving grace was that, at least this time, they did not try and use photographs of the shop for their own purposes.

A natural disaster, which hit significant parts of the whole country towards the end of our time in the shop, was the spread of Foot and Mouth Disease. We were surrounded by working farms and open countryside and the implications for local farms was immense. We felt that we should check with the Ministry of Agriculture, Fisheries and Food to see what, if anything, we should be doing, given that we had customers who came from a wide, surrounding area and who could, potentially, be carriers of the Disease. The advice from MAFF was that we did not need to provide disinfectant footbaths or anything as dramatic as that but that it would be advisable to ask customers not to bring their dogs to the shop any more. We had significant numbers of customers for whom a walk to the shop with their dogs was a regular part of their daily routine and we even had tethering rings outside the shop to which they could tie their dogs whilst they did their shopping. MAFF's rationale for their advice was that dogs walked or ran loose all over the countryside and they could be carriers for the Disease. Therefore it was preferable to keep the dogs apart from one another to minimise any spread. Accordingly, we put out a newsletter and displayed a notice in the shop asking our customers to heed this advice. The vast majority of our customers were only too happy to comply although some of them expressed the opinion that, given the mobility of the local wildlife, there was minimal risk of dogs being major carriers. There was, however, one memorable customer who became very aggressive when we politely asked her not to bring her dog to the shop for the immediate future. Her response was that, if that was how we felt, she would be cancelling her Sunday paper order, the only purchase she made from us, and she would take her custom elsewhere and with that she stormed out of the shop. We were completely taken aback by what appeared to us to be a completely selfish attitude and we concluded that it did not matter what we did in the shop, on this or any other matter, someone would always find fault! It was a great relief to everyone in the area when Foot and Mouth started to be contained and eventually died out without it affecting the village and the local vicinity. And it was a great relief to all the residents when they could once again bring their dogs down to the village shop!

One of the most tragic national events to occur whilst we were running the shop was the death of Diana, Princess of Wales, in 1997. We, together with millions of others, were completely overwhelmed by the occurrences which took place that night in Paris but the whole event had another, unanticipated, impact on us. When a tragedy such as this happens, it is natural for individuals to discuss it between themselves and their nearest and dearest. As shopkeepers who sold daily newspapers, the effect was magnified. Not only did every customer who came in want to discuss it with us but every newspaper we handled covered her death in every headline. The compound effect of all this on us, by the end of the day, was total physical and emotional exhaustion. It was a time of an extraordinary national outpouring of grief which was both heartfelt, and from our own small point of view, completely draining.

A less serious but equally unique event was the solar eclipse which occurred in 1999. Although widely predicted, nothing could have quite prepared us for the impact that this would have. It took place one August afternoon and, whilst we logically knew what was happening, we could quite appreciate why our ancient forebears would have been significantly affected by it. The most impressive feature, apart from a period of complete darkness in the middle of the afternoon, was the total silence. It appeared as though every creature was aware of what was happening. Birds were silent, animals in the fields were hushed, passing traffic ceased and not a soul came down to the shop. The eclipse only lasted a matter of minutes but its effect was profound.

Keith is interviewed by BBC Bristol at the opening of the refurbished shop

Sue and Keith sitting on the garden seat presented to them by the village at a surprise party following the sale of the shop

One of the earliest photographs of The Village Shop in Charlton Horethorne – known to be prior to 1905 as there is no telegraph pole outside the shop !

The Village Shop post-refurbishment in the late 1990's

Hitting the Headlines

We were very flattered by the press interest in our venture whilst we were carrying out the initial refurbishment of the shop but we were even more surprised to find that the interest continued. Just before we re-opened in July 1996, we had a telephone call from the BBC in Bristol saying that they would like to send a TV crew down to cover our opening morning. We were already apprehensive about our first day behind the counter and to make whatever faux pas we were going to make in front of the TV cameras seemed a little foolhardy. Nevertheless, we thought "what the hell" and agreed to be filmed. At about 9.00 a.m. on the morning in question, a cameraman, sound engineer and reporter arrived and we agreed that Keith would do the interview. When all was said and done, the whole process was fairly straightforward, once you got used to having a large, grey, furry microphone held under your chin! The questions were all about how we saw the future of village shops and what we hoped the future would hold for our particular shop. Keith got used to hearing the word "cut" when some noise, or customer, interrupted the interview but he was a bit disappointed when there was no sign of a "clapper board" nor did anyone shout "action"! The reporter then cornered a group of customers, including some children, and asked for some "spontaneous" response to the question "What do you think of your new shop?" "Spontaneous" was the intention, if not the result, as the question had to be repeated several times because the children were convulsed with giggles. We could not wait to close the shop to see our great TV debut and we rushed in to watch the local news. To give them their due, BBC Bristol did us proud and we videoed the broadcast so that we could watch our day of glory again if we wanted to. We were also under instruction from my father to record the programme as, much to his frustration, although my parents lived only four miles away, they were served by another local BBC station and he was unable to see us and our new venture as we hit the headlines.

We had received invaluable support and advice before and during our early days in the shop from ViRSA (Village Retail Services Association). We were therefore very flattered when one of the directors of ViRSA contacted us and asked if we would mind if they wrote an article about us and included it and a photo of the shop in their magazine. We happily agreed but we had no idea, at that stage, what this would lead to. In the early summer of 2001 we had a telephone call out of the blue from a researcher from The Saturday Times newspaper. The paper wanted to do a feature on successful village shops and, having seen the article about us in the ViRSA magazine, they asked if we would be prepared to be featured in a forthcoming colour supplement. We were thrilled and arranged for one of their photographers to come down on a Saturday morning. In the meantime, Keith was contacted, by the journalist who was writing the copy for the article, and he gave her an in-depth interview over the telephone.

In the days leading up to the photographer's visit, everything inside and outside the shop was given an extra thorough clean and the hanging baskets, planters outside the shop and the adjacent front garden of the cottage were weeded and dead-headed. On the Saturday morning we ordered in a special consignment of fresh fruit and vegetables and our baker, Roger Oxford, produced his full range of loaves, rolls and specialist savoury breads. When the photographer and his assistant arrived, they seemed to be very pleased with what they found, not least because it was a beautiful, sunny morning. They then spent the next couple of hours rearranging our stock in what they felt was a more photogenic display, including creating a display outside the shop on the forecourt. When they eventually finished, they endeared themselves to us even more by buying some things to take back with them to London. A couple of weeks later, the article was published and, to our delight, it was an excellent piece running to three pages in the colour supplement. Not only did it ensure that we sold out of The Times that Saturday, but it also had a knock-on effect on other sales. We had a succession of customers from far and wide who wanted to come and "see the shop that was in The Times". They also invariably wanted to buy a jar of Wicked Dark Chocolate Sauce, one of our special Dart Valley products, which had been featured in the article. We almost had a standing order with our supplier for weeks after the feature as it was nearly impossible to keep up with the demand!

Selling up and moving on

When we decided to buy the shop and go into business, we set ourselves a timescale of five to seven years, at the end of which we wanted to sell up and enjoy, hopefully, a long retirement. All the advice we received from fellow business people and professionals in the field was that it could take up to two years to sell a business. We also had the added complication that, to attract purchasers, we would have to sell our adjoining cottage as an integral part of the package to provide living accommodation for any future shop-owner. We thought long and hard about whether we would try to remain in the village after we had sold. There could be a downside to staying in Charlton Horethorne if the people we eventually sold to were not generally liked or they ran the shop in a way which the village was not happy with. Would we get the blame and could we bear to see what we had worked so hard at being allowed to run down again? After much discussion, we decided that, as we had made so many friends in the village and we had built up a lifestyle which we really enjoyed, we would take the risk and try to find another house in Charlton Horethorne. This was not going to be easy. Finding a house that we liked, we could afford and which came onto the market at the right time was going to be extremely difficult but at least our business ensured that we would probably be the first to hear about anyone in the village who was thinking of moving.

However, we solved our living accommodation conundrum, when, in the summer of 2000, a house called Quarry Cottage came on the market. The house, which was owned by an elderly couple, was actually only 30 years old and was named after a much older cottage which had previously stood on the site. To be perfectly honest, I was not too keen on the house when we first looked around. Bramble Cottage, our current house, had oak beams, an inglenook fireplace, a carved walnut staircase, thick walls and old windows with original, wonky glass, in other words, character. Quarry Cottage's décor was still in the '70's with polished-wood, open-tread stairs, a gold-coloured glass serving hatch from the kitchen to the dining area and kitchen and bathroom fittings which had definitely seen better days, in other words that dreaded word "potential" was raising its ugly head again.

After looking around the house a second time, we sat down and did some hard thinking. If we did not make an offer for Quarry Cottage we might not get the opportunity to buy another potentially suitable house in the village. However, we did not seem to be close to selling our existing house and the shop and did we really want to saddle ourselves with another house and a mortgage for an indeterminate period? Eventually we came to the conclusion that we should take the plunge and for the period until we sold the shop, we would let Quarry Cottage. So we went ahead and made an offer, which was accepted, and in early 2001 we became the proud owners of another house! As we had no prospective buyers on the horizon for the shop, we contacted a letting agent with a view to renting out our new house. They soon found us a very nice couple who had sold their own house and who were looking to buy in the area. They moved in and we went back to concentrating our efforts on selling the shop and cottage. At the same time we engaged our architect, Tim MacBean, yet again, to help us draw up the plans for the alterations we wanted to carry out to Quarry Cottage when we were in a position financially to proceed.

The first tenants in Quarry Cottage stayed until they found somewhere to buy and, when they moved out, the agent found us a family who were similarly looking for a property to purchase in the area. When they too were successful, we had a third couple, this time with a young child, and they rented the house until the end of July 2002. Earlier in the spring, we had agreed a specification of the work we wanted carried out at Quarry Cottage, with Tim MacBean, and he once more went out to tender on our behalf with a number of builders. We had decided that we would build an extension on the back of the house to give us a fourth bedroom and a separate dining room and that, together with the major overhaul of the house, meant that it was going to be quite a big building job. We were consistent in our decision-making and we again chose D.J. Chutter to carry out the work for us. Having decided not to let the house again, we instructed Chutters to start work in the early autumn of 2002. This instruction was very much on the basis that we agreed to certain defined areas of work and, when they were completed, we then approved the starting of another phase. We were very conscious that we still had not sold the business and we were therefore spending out of our savings until we found us a buyer.

In January 2001, we made our first attempt at selling the business. There was a popular monthly magazine in circulation called "Country Living" which had a section dedicated to the sale of country properties. We thought that we would have a go at selling privately, without using an agent, and we placed an advert in the magazine. We were very conscious of the effect that this could have, both on our staff and on the village, given the shop's past history and it would soon be common knowledge that we had bought another house in Charlton Horethorne. We therefore put out a newsletter to the village and had a meeting with our staff. Catherine and Sue were rather shocked but they were very supportive and we tried to reassure them that whatever happened it was not likely to happen very quickly and, in any event, we would do our utmost to try and secure their jobs with any new owner. Our customers were equally taken aback but equally supportive. The only problem we had was responding to the statement that "we hope you sell to someone nice"! We had a number of criteria which we hoped to fulfil, not least a purchaser with a healthy bank balance, but "niceness" was a little hard to quantify!

In any event, the "Country Living" advert came and went with very little response and we decided that we had better leave it to the experts. In March 2001, we appointed Palmer Snell, a local estate agent, which sold both domestic and business property. We were very encouraged by their enthusiasm for what we wanted to sell and particularly by the price that they said we could hope to achieve, which was quite a lot higher than we had anticipated. However, we soon learnt that anticipation and achievement are two totally different things. In four months we had absolutely no viewings and in July 2001 we changed agents. This time we selected an agent, Christies, whose entire business was devoted to selling commercial properties. Christies were not quite so optimistic about the price we would achieve and they warned us that the shop could take some time to sell as there would be a limited number of potential purchasers for a high quality, relatively highly priced business like ours. We were a little disappointed but not disheartened as Christies' approach did at least seem to be realistic.

In the spring of 2002 we did not seem to be making much progress on our sale and we arranged to go and meet Christies at their office in Winchester. We came away feeling decidedly unimpressed, both with the fact that the impetus on our sale seemed to have basically stalled and the agent who had been handling the promotion of our property had, unbeknown to us until that meeting, just left the company! We came back and did some more research and decided, once more, that we should change agents and we moved to Humberstones. From the very start they seemed to be much more proactive and we started to get viewings. One day, in the summer of 2002, we had a telephone call from Humberstones making arrangements for a family from Leicester to come and view the shop and cottage on a Saturday afternoon.

The family in question were a middle-aged couple called the Bakers, with two teenaged daughters. Both the husband and the wife had run their own businesses before, him in the house removal business and her in the estate agency business, and having sold both companies they decided they wanted to work together on a new project. They had some previous connections in the Weston-Super-Mare area and wanted to move to the West Country. They had both daughters with them when they viewed the property and we soon concluded that they would be a major attraction for all the young males in the area. They were both blonde and very attractive, although the younger one was extremely reluctant to move south and leave all her friends behind. We showed them around the cottage and then I took them around the shop. This turned out to be rather eventful. It was a warm summer's day and I was wearing sandals, which was a mistake. I was in full flow, describing some particularly interesting aspect of the shop when I caught my sandal on the corner of a shelving unit and I went flying onto the wooden floor. I ended up in a heap at their feet trying desperately to regain my composure and not let the extreme pain, that I was feeling in my knees, show! In retrospect it did seem a rather excessive gesture on my part to try and persuade them to buy the property! Nevertheless, it appeared to work. We were absolutely delighted when, following the viewing, we had a telephone call from the agent to say that the Bakers had made an offer of the full asking price for the shop and cottage. We were incredibly relieved and felt that, at last, we could start planning for the future.

The autumn was drifting towards winter and solicitors letters were still winging their way backwards and forwards but the progress did seem to be slowing down rather. One afternoon we received the telephone call that we had never wanted to receive. Our agent rang and said that the Bakers had pulled out. We were devastated and so was the agent. He had been unable to get any logical explanation for this change of mind but he assured us that he would redouble his efforts to find us a buyer. It was October, we had a builder who had already partly demolished our new home and, thinking that we could not commit a new owner to excessive expenditure, we had back-peddled on ordering any of our usual stock for Christmas. I think, in the whole six and a half years we had been in the shop, this was one of our lowest points but we decided that, as we were going to be running the shop for another Christmas, we were going to do it properly. It would only depress us even further if we had a drab, half-hearted Christmas and, anyway, a profitable Christmas would help finance the building work!

We did our very best to enjoy Christmas but we were worried. We even contemplated the scenario that we could not sell the shop and what were we going to do then? All the alternatives seemed unpalatable and we concluded that there was nothing we could do but carry on and believe our agent, Humberstones, when they said that it would eventually sell.

Humberstones, our agent, were as good as their word and we did have further interest in the spring of 2003, including a young couple who were very enthusiastic about buying the shop. They came from the London area and had owned and run a children's nursery which they were in the process of selling because they wanted to bring up their family out of London. They viewed the property twice and brought one set of parents with them as well as this was to be an extended family move. Our only real concern, apart from the fact that they still had not sold their own property, was that they had a very young family. The youngest child was only about eighteen months old, with two older ones of about four and six years. The mother said that she did not intend to work in the shop until the youngest child was at least two or three years old and, knowing the volume of work involved in running the shop, we could not see how the father was going to manage. However, they were keen and, after what had happened previously, we were pleased to have such positive interest.

Then something totally unexpected happened. Our agent telephoned and said that the Bakers had been in contact again and reinstated their full offer! We had very mixed emotions. On the one hand, we were delighted that we had a potential sale again but we were very cautious about getting too enthusiastic having been so badly let down before. We asked our agent to carry out extensive research into the validity of this offer and he came back saying that, as far as was possible to tell, there was no reason to doubt the genuineness of the offer. He also said that the Bakers wanted a quick completion. It was now May and they wanted to be in-situ by July! Despite our concerns about how they would cope with the business, we asked Humberstones to contact the young couple who were so enthusiastic and give them first refusal. Unfortunately, they still had not sold their business so we told Humberstones to accept the Baker's offer although we were still very sceptical about the eventual outcome.

As the weeks went on and everything seemed to be going ahead in a much more straightforward fashion than previously, we went back to Chutters and asked them to take the foot off the brake and put it on the accelerator! Given the uncertainty under which we, and they, had been labouring, they were very accommodating and we were back into arranging new kitchen fittings (courtesy of my stepson, Richard, who worked for Magnet at the time!), new bathroom fittings, choosing carpets and curtains etc., etc., etc. There was definitely a feeling of déjà vu! So much so that I said to Dave King, the foreman who had overseen the renovation of Bramble Cottage and who was still the foreman on our current job, that one day we would find a house that did not require all this work. His response was not altogether encouraging. He said "Well, you'd better get on with it!" I felt about ninety years old!

Anyway, this time everything went to plan and completion on the sale of the shop and Bramble Cottage was set for 18th July 2003. We organised a removal company and set about producing comprehensive notes, to help the Bakers when they moved in, on everything from suppliers, to account customers, to our Christmas arrangements and staffing issues. We were delighted when they said that they wished to keep Catherine and Sue and it was good to be able to tell them that their jobs were safe. However, Catherine had decided that she wanted to be more involved in her parents' farm and, whilst she agreed to stay for the handover, she moved on to her new role not long after we left. We also agreed that I would carry on running the Post Office for a couple of weeks after completion date as Richard Baker would have to go on a Post Office training course before he could take over and it would be impossible to complete this in the timescale. Work up at Quarry Cottage was continuing at a frenetic pace but it was clear that a lot of the internal painting work was not going to be completed by the time the carpets were due to be laid. To overcome this, Keith became a painter's mate in the afternoons, after working in the shop in the morning. He spent many hours sitting on the floor painting skirting boards to ensure the job was done.

On the due day, Catherine and Sue ran the shop whilst I saw furniture and boxes out of Bramble Cottage and Keith saw them into Quarry Cottage. I followed the furniture out of the house with the vacuum cleaner, cleaning liquid and dusters together with a lovely lady called Sarah McCormack, who normally helped my mother in her house but who had volunteered to help me on removal day. The last of our lorries had just left, on what was a scorching hot day, and Sarah and I were still on our knees cleaning in the kitchen (it is amazing what you find behind the dishwasher when it is moved!) when the Bakers and their lorries arrived. It was about 12.00 p.m. and we had still not had the telephone call from our solicitor to tell us that the money had come through for the sale. To be fair to them, the Bakers would not allow their lorries to unload until we received the call to say that the sale had been completed. Whilst we waited, the two Baker daughters leaned on the garden wall, wearing smart mini-skirts and tee shirts and flicking their long, blonde hair and the male population of Charlton Horethorne began to turn up in their droves! Still the waiting went on. Eventually, just before 2.00 p.m. we received the necessary telephone call, I handed the keys over and called a very relieved Keith on the mobile phone to tell him that the deal was done. So ended seven years, almost to the day, of hard work, fulfilled ambition and lifelong experience which we would not have missed for the world.

Postscript

A couple of months after we had sold the shop, we had a telephone call from Catherine to say that she and her husband, John, fancied a meal out at a local pub and would we like to join them? We had been up to our eyes since the move in settling into our new home and an evening out with friends, catching up on local gossip seemed like a good idea. Catherine said that she and John would come and pick us up. On the appointed evening, they came and collected us and we set off down into the village. I suppose we should have smelt a rat but we did not! Catherine and John pulled into the village hall and we realised that we had been had! We got out of the car and went into the hall to find well over a hundred of the village residents who had organised a surprise party for us. We were totally overwhelmed. We tried to speak to as many people as possible and then there was a call for silence. A speech of thanks was then given and we were presented with a beautiful, wooden garden bench, bearing a plaque of thanks from the village, and garden vouchers worth over £200. We were humbled and very emotional. We had come into this village to live a dream and the fact that what we had done was so appreciated is something that will live with us forever.

The Known History of Charlton Horethorne Village Shop and Post Office

At the turn of the 20th century, the village held various celebrations and these included an exhibition in the village hall of village memorabilia. For that exhibition we researched the history of Charlton Horethorne Village Shop and Post Office and the following is what we found out, updated with events up to 2007:

1869: The shop was first shown as "Post Office" and Mrs. Sarah Turner was appointed "Receiver" on 22nd February, which was probably the official opening date. Letters arrive from Sherborne by foot post and are delivered at 9.30 a.m., despatched at 3.30 p.m. week days only. Milborne Port is the nearest Money Order Office. (Mrs Turner was also the School Mistress.)

The main shop, which was the Drapery Store and Post Office, was run by Mrs. Sarah Turner from the 1860's; William Henry Pridham from the 1890's (certainly until 1906) and later by the Best family. A local informant states that Mr. Best, who ran the Post Office and Drapery Store, had retired from being the village policeman and it is possible that he held that post from 1899 to 1902.

[1] *Extracts from "The Story of Charlton Horethorne" by Robert Williams*

1871 Census:

Name	Relation	Age	Occupation
Sarah Turner	Widow	40	School Mistress
Thomas William	Son	16	Baker
Richard	Son	13	Post Office Assistant
George	Son	11	Scholar
Annie	Daughter	10	Scholar
Edward	Son	5	Scholar

1881 Census: 13 School Buildings

Name	Relation	Age	Occupation
Sarah Turner	Widow	51	School Mistress
George	Son	21	Carpenter
Annie	Daughter	19	Teacher
Edward	Son	15	Post Messenger
William H. Pridham		28	Grocer and Tea Dealer
Emily	Wife	30	
Harry	Son	1	
Mary A.	Mother	50	
Unnamed son		1 mth.	
Mary Jane Perry		17	General Domestic Servant

1894: Post and Money Order Office, Savings Bank and Annuity and Insurance Office. William Henry Pridham, Sub Postmaster. Letters arrive from Sherborne at 7.35 a.m.; despatched at 5.45 p.m. week days only Milborne Port railway station is the nearest Telegraph Office. [1]

1905: The installation of the Telegraph Office in this village resulted from a Parish Council request to the General Post Office in January 1905, following one made originally in 1898. It was installed following signature, on 29th April 1905, of a Deed of Arrangement between the Postmaster General and the Parish Council. [1]

Extract from *"My Childhood Days in Charlton Horethorne"* by Marion Trowbridge, 1990:

"The Post Office was much smaller then, of course there were no telephones in those days, the Postmaster would dial the telegrams. I can remember when the one came through to say the First World War was over. Mr. Best was the village policeman then, and when he gave up, he took over the Post Office and shop. The first telephone kiosk that came here was put inside the shop.

Mr. Best who kept the Post Office had two cars for hire and if we went to Yeovil or Sherborne he or his son would take us to Milborne Port.

I left school at the age of fourteen and started work at the Post Office and shop at the weekly wage of seven shillings and sixpence. The shop opened at eight, closed for an hour for dinner and then shut at seven. On Saturday the shop kept open until nine in the evening."

1935: The Parish Council wrote to the Head Postmaster to ask for the erection of a public kiosk outside the Post Office, as there was no public phone in the village when the Post Office was closed. [1]

1939 – 1971: The shop and Post Office was owned and run by Mr. and Mrs. Charles Peacock.

1972 – 1995: The shop and Post Office was leased by Mr. and Mrs. Peacock, firstly to the late Mr. and Mrs. Bill Cole from Newbury, then to the late Miss Caldwell and finally to the late Mr. Peter Lines.

1995 – 1996: Village volunteers ran the shop, with the help of temporary, stand-in postmistresses, whilst the property was on the market.

1996 – 2003: Sue and Keith Gudgeon bought, renovated and ran the shop and Post Office.

2003 – 2006: Julie and Richard Baker bought and ran the shop and Post Office.

2006 – Date: Sandy and Dave Wall bought and are running the shop and Post Office.